Fake Lao Tzu Quotes

Fake Lao Tzu Quotes
Erroneous Tao Te Ching Citations Examined

Stefan Stenudd

Stefan Stenudd is a Swedish author, artist, and historian of ideas. He has published a number of books in Swedish as well as English, both fiction and non-fiction. Among the latter are books about Taoism, the cosmology of the Greek philosophers, the Japanese martial arts, Tarot, astrology, and an encyclopedia of life force concepts.

His novels explore existential subjects from stoneage drama to science fiction, but lately stay more and more focused on the present. In the history of ideas he researches the thought patterns of creation myths, as well as Aristotle's *Poetics*. He is also an aikido instructor, 7 dan Aikikai, former Vice Chairman of the International Aikido Federation and Chairman of the Swedish Budo & Martial Arts Federation. He has his own extensive website:
stenudd.com

Books by Stefan Stenudd:
Ever Young, 2017, 2018, 2020.
Sunday Brunch with the World Maker, 2016, 2018, 2020.
All's End, 2007, 2015.
Occasionally I Contemplate Murder, 2006, 2011, 2015.
Cosmos of the Ancients: The Greek Philosophers on Myth and Cosmology, 2007, 2011, 2015.
Tao Te Ching: The Taoism of Lao Tzu Explained, 2011, 2015.
Tao Quotes, 2013, 2015.
Tarot Unfolded: Imaginative Reading of the Divination Cards, 2012, 2015.
Life Energy Encyclopedia, 2009, 2015.
Qi: Increase Your Life Energy, 2008, 2009, 2015.
Aikido Principles, 2008, 2016.
Attacks in Aikido, 2008, 2009, 2015.
Aikibatto: Sword Exercises for Aikido Students, 2007, 2009.
Your Health in Your Horoscope: Introduction to Medical Astrology, 2009, 2015.

Fake Lao Tzu Quotes:
Erroneous Tao Te Ching Citations Examined.
Copyright © Stefan Stenudd, 2020. All rights reserved.
Book design by the author.
ISBN: 978-91-7894-092-9
Publisher: Arriba, Malmö, Sweden, arriba.se

Contents

Introduction 9
Fake Lao Tzu quotes 18
A good traveler has no fixed plans 20
A man with outward courage 25
Act without expectation 28
An ant on the move 33
As soon as you have made a thought 35
At the center of your being 39
Be careful what you water your dreams 44
Be content with what you have 48
Because of a great love 51
Because one believes in oneself 54
Being deeply loved by someone 56
Can you step back from your own mind 58
Care about what other people think 61
Countless words count less 64
Do you imagine the universe is agitated? 68
Doing nothing is better 71
Embrace all things 73
Emptiness appears barren 77
Every human being's essential nature 81
Figure out the rhythm of life 84
From wonder into wonder 86
Give evil nothing to oppose 90
He who controls others 94
Health is the greatest possession 98
Highly evolved people 100

Hold your male side 102
Hope and fear are both phantoms 105
If a person seems wicked 108
If there is to be peace 110
If you are depressed 113
If you do not change direction 117
If you realize that all things change 119
If you want to awaken all of humanity 122
If you want to become whole 124
If you would take 126
Kindness in words 129
Knowing others 132
Knowledge is a treasure 135
Leadership 139
Life and death are one thread 142
Life is a series 146
Loss is not as bad 149
Love is a decision 154
Love is of all passions the strongest 156
Make your heart like a lake 158
Man's enemies are not demons 163
Marriage is three parts love 165
Most of the world's religions 167
Music in the soul 170
My teachings 174
Nature is not human-hearted 178
New beginnings 181
One cannot reflect 184
One who is too insistent 186
Perfect kindness 189
Quarrel with a friend 192
Respond intelligently 195
Silence is a source 198
Stop leaving 201

Stop thinking 205
Success is as dangerous as failure 208
The best fighter 210
The career of a sage 213
The flame that burns 215
The heart that gives 217
The key to growth 220
The moment truth is asserted 222
The past has no power 226
The reason why the universe is eternal 228
The snow goose need not bathe 232
The soul has no secret 235
The way to do 238
There are many paths 241
There is a time to live 244
There is no illusion 249
Time is a created thing 252
To a mind that is still 255
To hold 258
To see things in the seed 261
To understand the limitation 264
Violence, even well intentioned 267
Watch your thoughts 269
What the caterpillar calls the end 272
When I let go of what I am 275
When pure sincerity forms 277
When the student is ready 279
When you are content 285
When you find the way 287
Why do you run around 290
Your own positive future 292
Literature 296
Index 308

Introduction

In this Internet era, it is important to keep a skeptic mind to the sensational claims appearing on the web. That also goes for quotes from famous people of the present and the past. A popular meme jokes about this: Abraham Lincoln is quoted as saying that quotes on the Internet are often fake.

Indeed they are. One legendary mind of the past has been the victim of it more than most: Lao Tzu, the legendary first Taoist and author of *Tao Te Ching*. And that is far from only on the Internet. He has often been misquoted also in books, for the past hundred years or so.

Some of the fake quotes are close to what Lao Tzu stated in his book, whereas others are absurdly impossible to put in his mouth with any credibility. So, he is a good example of how a skeptical reader can go about testing a quote's authenticity, to whomever it is accredited.

We can learn also from words falsely claimed to be his. By recognizing the fakes, we get more familiar with what the true messages of Lao Tzu were, and how he worded them.

Lao Tzu and Tao Te Ching

Lao Tzu is the legendary writer of *Tao Te Ching* (*The Classic of the Way and Virtue*). He is supposed to have lived in the 6th century BC. Experts disagree on that dating – and even whether he ever existed. *Tao Te Ching* might be a compilation of separate texts and sayings, without one single author. But then again, it could also be that one man's work.

The name Lao Tzu is honorific. It means Old Master and has also been used traditionally as a title for the book *Tao Te Ching*. It is still the title preferred by many scholars.

The oldest manuscript of the book found so far is that from Guodian, dated to around 300 BC. It is far from complete, but its existence proves that the text appeared no later than in the 4th century BC. The oldest almost complete versions of the book are the two manuscripts found in Mawangdui, from around the year 200 BC, one slightly older than the other.

All other manuscripts are significantly more recent. The most widely spread and used version of *Tao Te Ching* has for many centuries been the one included in the comments to the text made by Wang Pi, who lived in the 3rd century CE. Its dominance all through to the 1970's is shown by sinologists calling it the transmitted text. It is even now the standard version translators weigh the heaviest upon.

Tao Te Ching is the foremost and oldest Taoist text. Originally, it had no division into 81 chapters. This was introduced later, probably in the 1st century BC. The number of chapters was established to create the symbolic symmetry of 9 X 9.

Already in the Mawangdui manuscripts, the book had two parts – although in both those manuscripts the order of them was reverse to the presently accepted form. The book's name is derived from these two parts. The first one starts with the word *Tao*, the Way, and the second part with *Te*, virtue (actually it starts with the expression "highest virtue").

Most of the chapters are at least partially rhymed. This was easily accomplished in the Chinese language and with its generous rules for what is considered a rhyme. Translations into other languages rarely try the same, at least not those produced since a few decades into the 20th century.

There have been countless translations of *Tao Te Ching*. In the Western world, the first one was made by the French priest Francois Noël in the beginning of the 18th century. It was in Latin and passed unnoticed. The first printed version was in French, by Stanislas Julien in 1842. In English, John Chalmers was the first in 1868. Already by the turn of the century, many other translations into several languages had followed.

Nowadays, there are hundreds in the English language alone.

Transcription

Chinese words are transcribed to Western languages in different ways. English *Tao Te Ching* versions mostly use the Wade-Giles system. Lately, the pinyin system, introduced by the Chinese government in the 1950's, is increasingly used – certainly for modern texts, but also to some extent for the Chinese classics.

Tao Te Ching is the Wade-Giles spelling. In pinyin it would be *Daodejing*. Lao Tzu is spelled Laozi in pinyin, but there have also been several other ways of spelling his name, for example Lao Tsu and Lao Tse.

In this book I use the Wade-Giles spelling, except for modern Chinese names or places, where I use pinyin. When quoting other texts, I use their spelling. It may seem confusing, but the differences are not bigger than that the words are easily recognized.

One certain but cryptic source to Lao Tzu

The only words that we know are those of Lao Tzu are in *Tao Te Ching* – and it is not even established beyond a doubt that the text had him or anyone else as the sole author. Other texts of Chinese antiquity and later have claimed to quote him, but that can often be debated, to say the least. So, a quote claiming with any certainty to be of Lao Tzu really needs to be from that book.

Tao Te Ching, composed somewhere between the 6th and the 4th century BC, is not an easy one to interpret – neither for the modern Chinese reader nor for those approaching it through a translation. Lao Tzu has a reputation of having been cryptic, although he spoke seemingly plainly and directly in his text. Furthermore, the ancient Chinese grammar – or rather lack of it – makes for many uncertainties. Even the punctuation is quite scarce in the text.

The obscurities of *Tao Te Ching* have made the many translations of the text go in all kinds of directions. Its cryptic nature has been an excuse for many translators to allow themselves deviations from the original wording, mostly with the purpose of making the book understandable to a modern audience.

In some cases it has gone too far for the word 'translation' to be accurate. The expression 'loosely based,' used in fiction, would be more adequate.

Variations of the first sentence of Tao Te Ching

A good example of this variety of interpretations is evident already in the first chapter of *Tao Te Ching* – from the very first sentence. If you want to get a hint on how reliable a translation is, just have a look at the first sentence, and you'll get a good indication.

On my Taoism website (taoistic.com), I have a page with 76 English versions of the first chapter. They have many similarities, but they also differ a lot.

If we stick to just the first few words of the chapter, which can be said to be the first sentence, the direct word by word translation reads:

Way can way not eternal way.

That makes little sense, before knowing that the word *Tao*, Way, can be both a noun and a verb – a way or "way-ing," which means using the way to go someplace. I translated it to "walking" in my version of *Tao Te Ching*, but any means of transport on the way would be alright.

A fitting generic term is "travel", but Lao Tzu – who made quite a few jokes in his text – enjoyed the wordplay, so the alliteration of walking the Way would be right up his alley, so to speak.

Some translators, James Legge being one of them, sticking with "Tao" instead of translating it, use "trodden", which is pretty much the same aspiration.

Well, I chose to translate *Tao* to the Way, and therefore my version of that first line is:

The Way that can be walked is not the eternal Way.

I dare say it can't be that far from Lao Tzu's intention. He speaks about a way not for walking. Indeed, it's the very Way of the whole world, how it emerged out of a mysterious primordial state and still directs everything happening here.

A very common translation of the line is:

The Tao that can be told is not the eternal Tao.

That alternative is indeed possible for the complex term *Tao* and all that it suggests. I just feel it misses the pun.

Most translations play with this paradox of sorts, but they have very different wordings of it. For example:

- Who would follow the Way must go beyond words.
- Nature can never be completely described, for such a description of Nature would have to duplicate Nature.
- Existence is beyond the power of words to define.
- The Tao that can be described is not the eternal Tao.
- A way can be a guide, but not a fixed path.
- The Tao that can be understood cannot be the primal, or cosmic, Tao.
- The Way that can be experienced is not true.
- Even the finest teaching is not the Tao itself.
- The Tao that refers to here can never be the mundane Tao.
- The Reason that can be reasoned is not the eternal Reason.
- There are many ways but the Way is uncharted.
- The principle that can be enunciated is not the one that always was.
- The infinity that can be conceived is not the everlasting Infinity.
- A path is just a path.

That's just the very first line of *Tao Te Ching*. So, interpretations of Lao Tzu's words can take all kinds of turns.

What makes some Lao Tzu quotes fake

Still, I would say some translations are more accurate than others. And some are so off, they must be deemed fake.

For example, we should expect a translation of any classic to stay true to its context and historical framework as much as possible. If a translation deviates so far from the original that it would be impossible to comprehend in the time it was originally written, then it may be accessible to modern readers – but what they read is a falsification.

Also, with such an obscure text as that of Lao Tzu, who can claim to know what would be a modern equivalent of it? Better to be faithful to the original wording.

A translation should be done with this principle always in mind: Stay as close to the original wording as possible, and deviate from it only when the language it is translated to demands it.

The place to explain and clarify for the modern reader is not in the translated text, but in comments and notes to it.

This is important not only out of respect for the original text, but just as much for the modern reader. Who would not be furious when afterwards realizing that the version on which one has based the judgment and understanding of a text is really a very free interpretation of it, or paraphrasing gone awry?

A reader turning to Lao Tzu wants to get as near to his thoughts as possible – not the thoughts of another, claiming to know what Lao Tzu "really" meant. It is for the reader to make that judgment, based on as accurate a translation as possible. Any help with this process should be in comments and such. Not in the translation of the Lao Tzu text.

Sadly, I have found that many of the fake Lao Tzu quotes originate in books with flawed translations of his text. In their eagerness to either clarify what they think Lao Tzu meant or to squeeze his words into a modern context, they have gone so far from the original wording of *Tao Te Ching* that their versions are misleading. They don't transmit the thoughts of Lao Tzu.

That's why quotes from such versions must be deemed falsely attributed to Lao Tzu. These quotes should instead be attributed to the translators in question. At best, it could be called paraphrasing, but not translation.

I have also found a number of so-called Lao Tzu quotes that are not traceable to existing translations of *Tao Te Ching*. Where they really originate is often hard to trace. Many of them come from completely different texts by other authors. In some cases, I have been unable to track their origins.

It would be interesting to know the source, but it is still much more important to establish that Lao Tzu was not the originator. His text is accessible in several very competent translations. There is no need to force new sayings into his mouth.

How to know what's fake and what's not

It is not easy for the reader to decide what is and is not a genuine Lao Tzu quote. But I hope that the examples I examine in this book of fake Lao Tzu quotes will give some clues.

Generally speaking, a Lao Tzu quote lacking reference to which of the 81 *Tao Te Ching* chapters it is from should be treated with initial doubt. If there is a chapter given, there is still reason for doubt. You need to know what translation has been used. Then there is the problem of many translations being sadly inaccurate...

Another way to go about it is to consider if the quote

makes sense, coming from a Chinese thinker living more than two thousand years ago. Most fake Lao Tzu quotes can be revealed because they use modern concepts, or reek of psychology, New Age, greeting card sentiments, motivational speech, mindfulness, and other perspectives unknown in the days of ancient China.

Many fake Lao Tzu quotes sound much more like Buddhist sayings, often close to Zen. But he lived many hundreds of years before Buddhism was introduced to China.

Another giveaway is religion. Lao Tzu cannot be described as a religious thinker. He was quite down-to-earth. He mentioned deities only twice in *Tao Te Ching*, and that was in passing (chapter 4 and 39). Nor did he ponder an afterlife, though he did mention ghosts of ancestors (chapter 60).

I have seen many fake Lao Tzu quotes suggest something you should do to improve your own life and develop your personal character. That's not really his thinking. His view was society as a whole, not some spiritual career of the individual. And he did not think, as we too often do, that some people got it while others don't and never will. He thought it was simply a question of understanding, and none would be inadequately equipped to do that.

The best method to reveal fake Lao Tzu quotes is to start by having a look at a competent translation of his text. You will quickly get a sense of what he was all about. There are several of those. Check my commented list of *Tao Te Ching* literature at the end of this book.

You will also notice what versions I tend to use for reference, when discussing the quotes. Those are, of course, widely respected translations that I deem trustworthy.

I'd like to think that my own translation, which I often use for comparison, is also trustworthy. But don't take my word for it.

Fake Lao Tzu quotes

In the following, I examine a number of fake Lao Tzu quotes circulating on the Internet. I have mostly chosen quotes that exist in *meme* form (image with text), because they tend to spread the most all over the web, especially in social media.

With each such quote I discuss why it must be deemed fake, or at least misleadingly flawed, and try to trace its true origin. For comparison, I mostly use my own version of *Tao Te Ching*, but also frequently translations that are generally regarded as knowledgeable and trustworthy.

All quotes treated have their own chapter, titled after their first words, and the chapters are alphabetically ordered for the reader's convenience. There is no particular point in reading them in this order. Just go where your curiosity leads you, or use this book as a reference when you come across Lao Tzu quotes that you feel doubtful about.

Notice that I have only chosen quotes that for some or other reason badly represent the thoughts of Lao Tzu as seen in *Tao Te Ching*. There are also many quotes on the web, in memes and plain text, truly or at least decently representing Lao Tzu's words. I am not sure that they are in majority or spread the most, which is saddening, but let's hope they will be the ones lasting.

As for the fake quotes, I don't presume to have treated all of the existing ones in this book. But I believe that I have caught just about all of those that have spread the most – so far. There will most probably be more of them popping up, on the web as well as in books using the web as a source for Lao Tzu quotes to decorate their texts.

My hope is that this book will assist readers in seeing the difference between true and fake Lao Tzu quotes, whether they are treated in the book or not. Also, I think this exploration will increase the reader's understanding of what the Taoism of Lao Tzu was really all about.

A good traveler has no fixed plans

"A good traveler has no fixed plans and is not intent on arriving."

Lao Tzu would probably be sympathetic towards such an attitude. In his view, plans should be made with caution and with high adaptability to circumstances as they evolve. One should not assume that one will arrive as intended.

He had his doubts about travel in general. In chapter 47 he stated (my version):

The longer you travel, the less you know.

And in chapter 80 he praised staying in one's own village, not even bothering to visit neighboring villages, although they were so near that roosters and dogs could be heard from there.

But the quote discussed here is not from *Tao Te Ching* – well, not a faithful translation of it.

It is from Stephen Mitchell's very popular 1988 version of the text, the beginning of chapter 27 (page 27), with the only difference being that Mitchell wrote "upon" instead of "on." On the Internet, the simplified spelling has triumphed over Mitchell's. A Google search shows about 50 times more results for the former than for the latter.

But it is a mystery how Mitchell got to this interpretation. My version for the same part of the chapter is:

A good wanderer leaves no trace.

James Legge's 1891 version reads (page 70):

The skilful traveller leaves no traces of his wheels or footsteps.

Robert G. Henricks writes in his 1989 translation (page 240):

The good traveler leaves no track behind.

So, it is about travel, but not about the destination. One should cover one's tracks, so to speak, and people will be unaware of from where one came.

Mitchell takes many great liberties in his whole version of *Tao Te Ching*. Also the next couple of lines in chapter 27 deviate considerably from the original:

A good artist lets his intuition
lead him wherever it wants.
A good scientist has freed himself of concepts
and keeps his mind open to what is.

Here is my version of the same part:

A good speaker does not stutter.
A good counter needs no calculator.
A good door needs no lock,
Still it can't be opened.
A good mooring needs no knot,
Still no one can untie it.

And that of Henricks:

The good speaker [speaks] without blemish or flaw;
The good counter doesn't use tallies or chips;
The good closer of doors does so without bolt or lock, and
yet the door cannot be opened;
The good tier of knots ties without rope or cord, yet his
knots can't be undone.

So, there is nothing about artists and intuition, or scientists and concepts, in Lao Tzu's text. Nothing of what it does mention – speakers, counters, doors, and knots – is included in Mitchell's version.

Mitchell does indeed take his poetic license very far. His text is charming, but frequently quite distant from Lao Tzu. Several fake Lao Tzu quotes discussed in this book originate in his version of *Tao Te Ching*. This is sad, since his version has been a bestseller through the decades since its original publication. That means lots of people have their opinion of Lao Tzu from his interpretation, although it is often closer to Mitchell than to Lao Tzu.

Stephen Mitchell is a US writer with a Zen training background, who has also written his own versions of *Gilgamesh*, *The Iliad*, *Bhagavad Gita*, and several other classics. His own website bio (stephenmitchellbooks.com/about/) is unusually short. He has studied at Amherst, Sorbonne, and Yale, which is impressive, but he neglects to mention what he studied – probably because then he "de-educated through intensive Zen practice."

In the foreword to his *Tao Te Ching*, Mitchell explained that he mainly used the version by Paul Carus from 1898, *Lao-Tze's Tao-Teh-King*, where the Chinese text is translated to English word by word, but also consulted "dozens of translations into English, German, and French." He added (page x):

> *But the most essential preparation for my work was a fourteen-year-long course of Zen training, which brought me face to face with Lao-tzu and his true disciples and heirs, the early Chinese Zen Masters.*

That is a strange choice, making Lao Tzu a Zen teacher although Buddhism did not reach China until hundreds of years after his time. For *Chán* (Zen in Chinese) it did not happen until the 5th or 6th century CE, as legend has it with the monk Bodhidharma. By that time Lao Tzu had been a revered thinker in China for at least 800 years and Taoism was a well established school of thought, with many disciples of its own.

There are indeed similarities between Taoism and Zen, but interpreting Lao Tzu through a Zen filter risk missing the differences.

By the way, the Carus version, with each Chinese word translated separately, supports completely the standard versions of the part of chapter 27 discussed here. It gives no support for Mitchell's wording. Here is the Carus word by word version (pages 187-188):

> *Good walkers have no rut [and] track.*
> *Good speakers have no blemish [and] error.*
> *Good counters have no counting bamboo slips.*
> *Good lockers have no bolts [and] keys, and not one can open [their locks].*
> *Good binders have no rope [and] string, and not one can loosen [their knots].*

Mitchell's *Tao Te Ching* is still (August 2020), after all these years, the most popular version of the book. Its influence on popular conception of Lao Tzu's thoughts is considerable, which is particularly obvious on the web, but also in books touching on the subject of Taoism.

His version is easy to admire for its clarity and elegance. But it is, as stated above, frequently far from standard interpretations of the Chinese original. In this book, there are several questionable Lao Tzu quotes coming from his version.

What impresses me most with his book is the straightforward simplicity of his wordings, and what bothers me the most is their considerable deviation from Lao Tzu's philosophy. In short, his version is more Stephen Mitchell than Lao Tzu. That is a pity, because readers are not properly made aware of it.

Quotes from Stephen Mitchell's *Tao Te Ching* are discussed in a number of other chapters in this book. Here they all are:

"Act without expectation"
"Be content with what you have"
"Because of a great love"
"Can you step back from your own mind"
"Care about what other people think"
"Give evil nothing to oppose"
"Hope and fear are both phantoms"
"If you realize that all things change"
"If you want to become whole"
"Knowing others"
"Man's enemies are not demons"
"My teachings"
"Stop thinking"
"Success is as dangerous as failure"
"There is a time to live"
"There is no illusion"
"Violence, even well intentioned"
"When you are content"

A man with outward courage

"A man with outward courage dares to die; a man with inner courage dares to live."

This is a strange statement. Inner courage can be understood as a psyche able to be courageous, which is the same as plainly saying courage. Where else would the courage be, if not in a person's inner conditions? But then, outward courage can be nothing but the expression of that inner capacity. So, they can hardly differ in nature.

What might be intended is the difference between courage in deeds and courage in thought. Certainly, people who regard themselves as courageous can fail when put to the test, whereas many cowards show great bravery in times of crisis. But that would not explain how one leads to death and the other to life.

If it's about being a daredevil, putting oneself in danger to impress others by showing courage, then it would make more sense to say that the courageous dare to die, and the cowardly dare to live. But that has less of a glorious flare about it.

The message of the quote could be sort of psychoanalytical. It is easier to die in a bold deed than to seek and examine one's inner flaws. That has proven to be true in many cases of abrupt self-sacrifice. Some people have willingly met their own death rather than living on with their inner torments, much less facing them.

In any case, Lao Tzu would not divide courage into an

outward and an inner form. But he did write about two expressions of courage leading to those extremes in the outcome. It is in chapter 73 of *Tao Te Ching*. Here is my version:

Those who have the courage to dare will perish.
Those who have the courage not to dare will live.

Here is D. C. Lau's version from 1963 (page 135):

He who is fearless in being bold will meet with his death;
He who is fearless in being timid will stay alive.

So, it is not about what kind of courage one has, but how it is expressed, to what action it leads or doesn't lead. Those who dare to resist challenges to their courage will survive.

The difference between the quote discussed here and Lao Tzu's words may seem minute, but it makes a huge difference in how the words are to be understood.

Still, there is an English version of *Tao Te Ching* that contains the quote in chapter 73, but with the use of "inward" instead of "inner." It is Witter Bynner's book *The Way of Life According to Laotzu: An American Version* from 1944 (page 71):

A man with outward courage dares to die,
A man with inward courage dares to live.

The American poet Witter Bynner (1881-1968) also translated old Chinese poetry in a long-time collaboration with Kiang Kang-hu, a professor of Chinese. His often somewhat odd interpretation of Lao Tzu's words is the source to several misleading Lao Tzu quotes on the Internet – and in an increasing number of books. Being a poet himself, he must have allowed himself quite a dose of poetic license, which is probably the reason for the subtitle *An American Version*.

Not knowing the Chinese language, he based his version on a number of extant translations – as any translator of a classic text, whether familiar with the language or not, needs to do – and explained in the introduction (page 15): "Laotzu should, I am convinced, be brought close to people in their own idiom, as a being beyond race or age."

It is a praiseworthy ambition, but it brings the risk of deviating so far from the original intentions of the text that it gets closer to the translator than to Lao Tzu. The best translation of this classic is such that the readers experience at least some of the ancient Chinese context and are trusted to do some translating of their own, so to speak, into "their own idiom." Lao Tzu spoke to his contemporaries. If that is removed, readers are robbed of the possibility to draw their own conclusions as to how his words can be relevant today.

It is not like *Tao Te Ching* was that easy to understand at the time and place of its emergence, either. Its obscurity contributes significantly to its continued attraction.

Here are the other chapters of this book where Witter Bynner's version of *Tao Te Ching* is discussed: "At the center of your being," "From wonder into wonder," and "The way to do."

Act without expectation

"Act without expectation."

One wonders – expectation of what? A common expression is "act without expectation of reward," but if we expect no result at all from our actions, there is no reason to act. And if we don't know what to expect, then we should be very careful when acting – again probably do best to avoid it altogether.

That would actually be right up Lao Tzu's alley. He argued for *wu-wei*, non-action. Still, that does not mean never doing anything, but doing as little as possible in order to avoid doing too much.

He understood that action was sometimes needed, but it should be done with great care and hesitation. If things could be left to solve themselves, which he meant was often the case, then indeed we should refrain from acting. He explained it like this in chapter 43 (n my version):

> *The softest in the world*
> *Surpasses the hardest in the world.*
> *What has no substance*
> *Can penetrate what has no opening.*
> *Thereby I know the value of non-action.*

So, action – when needed – should be soft and discreet, making as little of a mark as possible. Then it will meet no resistance and actually succeed to solve the problem at hand, no matter how big it is.

To Lao Tzu, then, it is not about expectance, but about sensitivity and moderation. Chapter 59 states:

When leading people and serving Heaven,
Nothing exceeds moderation.
Truly, moderation means prevention.
Prevention means achieving much virtue.

When much virtue is achieved,
Nothing is not overcome.

The quote examined here is too short, too absolute, to fit Lao Tzu's philosophy. Either it is simply not a quote of his, or it's taken out of context. The latter is the case, because there are versions of *Tao Te Ching* that have this phrase – but not on its own.

The oldest book connecting the exact quote examined here to Lao Tzu is the 1986 version of *Tao Te Ching* by R. L. Wing, *The Tao of Power*, which ends chapter 77 (no pagination):

Therefore evolved individuals
Act without expectation,
Succeed without taking credit,
And have no desire to display their excellence.

His wording is not that far from the usual. Here is my version of the same lines:

Therefore, the sage acts without taking credit.
He accomplishes without dwelling on it.
He does not want to display his worth.

Here is that of James Legge from 1891 (page 119):

> *Therefore the (ruling) sage acts without claiming the results as his; he achieves his merit and does not rest (arrogantly) in it; — he does not wish to display his superiority.*

Philip J. Ivanhoe in his 2002 translation had this wording (page 80):

> *This is why sages act with no expectation of reward.*
> *When their work is done, they do not linger.*
> *They do not desire to make a display of their worthiness.*

I do not like Wing's choice of "evolved individuals" instead of "the sage," since it is a modern concept, with some ugly connotations at that. Would some people be more evolved than others? That flawed thinking belongs to a recent period of human thought we are happy to have left behind.

As for the quote examined here, one might regard "act without expectation" as a way of expressing the noble mind of not expecting praise, but on its own it is misleading. The statement is in need of one or two clarifying words. Lao Tzu's meaning was definitely not that the sage would act expecting no result.

Other books have used Wing's version of the quote, bringing their own context to it. An odd example of this is *Thinking Body, Dancing Mind: TaoSports for Extraordinary Performance in Athletics, Business, and Life* from 1992, by Chungliang Al Huang and Jerry Lynch. I doubt that Lao Tzu would have been pleased with the term TaoSports. They dedicated their book to the Jungian mythologist Joseph Campbell "who, as a world-class runner, personified the TaoAthlete" (page v). It is not really what made Campbell famous.

Anyway, they used the quote to illustrate the need not to tie oneself to expectations or preconceived notions, thereby: "You, like a samurai warrior, expect nothing and become ready for everything" (page 132). It is odd linking the Chinese thinker Lao Tzu to the Japanese warrior class, but their use of *mushin*, empty mind, comes closer to the idea of acting without expectation than anything he said.

The book *One Heart: Universal Wisdom from the World's Scriptures* from 2004, edited by Bonnie Louise Kuchler, used a version slightly different from that of Wing (page 16):

Therefore the wise act without expectation,
do not abide in their accomplishments,
do not want to show their virtue.

I am happy to see "evolved individuals" replaced by "the wise," which is of course synonymous with "the sage." The problem remains, though, with the words "without expectation," implying a lack of care about results.

What version of *Tao Te Ching* Kuchler used for this quote is a mystery. It is not in any of the nine versions listed in the bibliography of the book. Nor have I found it anywhere else. The closest I have come is Charles Muller's version on his own website (acmuller.net) and in the 2005 book with his translation of *Tao Te Ching*:

Therefore the sage acts without expectation.
Does not abide in his accomplishments.
Does not want to show his virtue.

That is probably the one used by Kuchler, with minor edits. The problem of "without expectation" is there as well, although Muller is an accomplished translator, indeed, and an expert on East Asian philosophy and religion.

For more on Charles Muller's version of *Tao Te Ching*, see the chapter "Loss is not as bad."

Stephen Mitchell also used "without expectation" in his very popular version of *Tao Te Ching* from 1988. Speaking about the Master, he used "she" in this chapter, since he altered the gender in the chapters to avoid the male stereotype – and the Chinese text does not specify any gender. That is admirable. Here is his rendition of the last lines of chapter 77 (page 77):

She acts without expectation,
succeeds without taking credit,
and doesn't think that she is better
than anyone else.

His solution, too, contains the problem with no expectation. For more about Stephen Mitchell and his version of *Tao Te Ching*, see the chapter "A good traveler has no fixed plans."

They would all have done better to use the familiar expression of acting without expectation of reward.

An ant on the move

"An ant on the move does more than a dozing ox."

There is no ant in *Tao Te Ching*, nor is there an ox except for a "feast of the ox" mentioned in chapter 20, which was the *t'ai-lao* sacrifice at spring. The saying here is humorous, but Lao Tzu would probably have frowned at it. His message of *wu-wei*, non-action, was closer to the dozing ox than the ant on the move.

The oldest book I have found with this exact quote is *Folk Wisdom of Mexico* from 1994, by Jeff M. Sellers (page 36). It is called an anonymous Mexican proverb. Other books published later have also used the quote, describing it as a Mexican proverb.

In 2006, though, the Reader's Digest book *Treasury of Wit & Wisdom* edited by Jeff Bredenberg presented the quote as from Lao Tzu (page 130). The book also contains a short text about Lao Tzu (page 74) and several other quotes ascribed to him. Many of them are questionable, to say the least. Others are plausible, and the main source to them seems to be Wing-tsit Chan's 1963 version of *Tao Te Ching* – but there certainly is no ant on the move or dozing ox in it.

It is hard to see how Bredenberg could make the mistake of ascribing a Mexican proverb to Lao Tzu, but there it is. And several books that followed inherited the mistake – not to mention plenty of web pages and memes.

The oldest web page I have found containing the quote, with an ascertained date, is a blog post from August 7, 2008, accrediting it to Lao Tzu. On Facebook, the quote didn't appear until February 2012 – in two posts, none ascribing the quote to anyone. The following year there was a post by Sunwarrior healthfood with a meme, ascribing the quote to Lao Tzu.

Not only Lao Tzu has been ascribed to the quote. On Goodreads, there is a listing of it as a Zen proverb. I even came across a web page accrediting it to Mike Tyson.

As soon as you have made a thought

"As soon as you have made a thought, laugh at it."

My first reaction to this quote was: do you make a thought, isn't it so that you have it? We will get to that, but let's start with the message of this quote as it is written and what it suggests. Should you laugh at a thought that appears in your mind, whatever it is? That's like saying you should reject all your thinking. It will not get you anywhere.

It is by thinking we can begin to understand the world in which we live. If we discard thinking just because it is a thought, then we realize nothing. Lao Tzu was not opposed to thinking. What he regarded with suspicion was knowledge, the attitude of being certain about things by being learned. Chapter 48 of *Tao Te Ching* says (my version):

> *Those who seek knowledge,*
> *Collect something every day.*
> *Those who seek the Way,*
> *Let go of something every day.*

And chapter 71 starts with this clear statement:

> *Knowing that you do not know is the best.*
> *Not knowing that you do not know is an illness.*

He made a distinction between knowing and knowledge. The former is the mind reaching conclusions – or realizing that it cannot. The latter is an unprocessed quantity, gathering and memorizing a lot of information without properly digesting it. In the 81st and last chapter, Lao Tzu spoke of the difference between knowing and being learned:

Those who know are not learned.
Those who are learned do not know.

As for laughter, he was indeed no stranger to humor. *Tao Te Ching* is full of it, playing with words, using amusing paradoxes, and so on. But laughter per se he only mentioned once, in chapter 41, when speaking about people's differing attitudes towards teachings of *Tao*, the Way:

The superior student listens to the Way
And follows it closely.
The average student listens to the Way
And follows some and some not.
The lesser student listens to the Way
And laughs out loud.
If there were no laughter it would not be the Way.

Notice, though, that this laughter is a sign of folly, and not at all some enlightened reaction to thoughts about the Way.

The earliest appearance I have found of this exact quote in a book is in *Fellini on Fellini*, a collection of texts by the movie director Federico Fellini translated by Isabel Quigley, from 1976. It says, in regard to Fellini's 1970 film *The Clowns* (page 124):

Wasn't St. Francis known as God's clown? And didn't Lao Tse say: 'As soon as you have made a thought, laugh at it'?

This is from an essay by Fellini called "Un viaggio nell'ombra" ("A journey into the shadows") in *I clowns*, edited by Renzo Renzi, from 1970. I have not been able to check the Italian text, but it is possible that Fellini might have misinterpreted the line about laughter in chapter 41, quoted above.

The next book with the quote is *Silver Departures: a Collection of Quotations* from 1983, by Richard Kehl, ascribing the quote to Lao Tzu (page 40). Kehl might have gotten it from the Fellini book, but he gave no information about it.

The oldest appearance of the quote I have found on the Internet is a blog post from October 2006 by the writer Roger von Oech, accrediting it to Lao Tzu. He had previously published the quote in his book *A Whack on the Side of the Head* in its 1990 edition (page 91), but not in the first edition from 1983. Therefore, I find it likely that he got the quote from Kehl's book mentioned above.

Now, let us move on to a shorter version of the quote that makes more grammatical sense:

As soon as you have a thought, laugh at it.

This quote is less spread, but it is also accredited to Lao Tzu. The earliest book I have found to include it is *The Four Purposes of Life* from 2011, by Dan Millman (page 23). It is possible that he paraphrased Kehl or von Oech.

On the web I have found one occurrence of the quote older than Millman's book. It is in a column by Joey Garcia in a Sacramento news website, already from February 26, 2004. She accredited it to Lao Tzu. It would be very interesting to know where she got it from, since it cannot have been Millman. Being a journalist, she might have seen the quote with "made a thought" and edited it, which is totally understandable.

So, I have to settle for the most plausible source to this false Lao Tzu quote being Fellini. It could be worse.

At the center of your being

"At the center of your being you have the answer; you know who you are and you know what you want."

This fake Lao Tzu quote is not only questionable with its use of the semi-colon. I see nothing in it relating to the ideas of Lao Tzu.

He would reject the whole idea of what you want, focusing instead on what you need. You are likely to find out what you want when you get it, and not before, but Lao Tzu would probably suggest that you are most likely to get what you need if you ignore what you want.

The center of your being is also something alien to Lao Tzu, as is contemplating who you are. That's all *Tao*, the inner workings of the world and everything in it. Lao Tzu expressed one fundamental cure for mankind: returning to the Way, the natural state of things. He did not see it as some kind of soul-searching.

The quote is part of a full poem, appearing in the 1994 book *A Grateful Heart: Daily Blessings for the Evening Meal from Buddha to the Beatles,* by M. J. Ryan. Here it is in its entirety (pages 248-249):

Always we hope
someone else has the answer.
Some other place will be better,
some other time
it will turn out.

This is it.
No one else has the answer.
No other place will be better,
and it has already turned out.

At the center of your being, you have the answer;
you know who you are and you know what you want.

There is no need
to run outside
for better seeing.

Nor to peer from a window.

Rather abide at
the center of your being;
for the more you leave it
the less you learn.

Search your heart
and see
the way to do
is to be.

M. J. Ryan claims that it is Lao Tzu, but with "translator unknown." In the copyright acknowledgements she mentions two *Tao Te Ching* translations (page 264), but it is from neither. Part of the quote can be found in the version by Witter Bynner: *The Way of Life according to Laotzu* from 1944. The second part of the poem, starting "There is no need," is his rather free version of chapter 47, though missing his next to last line: *"If he is wise who takes each turn:"* Also, Bynner used fewer line breaks. Ryan must have wanted to accentuate the poetic flair of the quote, but by those line breaks she hid the fact that Bynner's version is rhymed (page 55):

There is no need to run outside
For better seeing,
Nor to peer from a window. Rather abide
At the center of your being;
For the more you leave it, the less you learn.
Search your heart and see
If he is wise who takes each turn:
The way to do is to be.

Here is my version of that *Tao Te Ching* chapter:

Without stepping out the door,
You can know the world.
Without looking through the window,
You can see Heaven's Way.
The longer you travel, the less you know.
Therefore:
The sage knows without traveling,
Perceives without looking,
Completes without acting.

The first part of the poem in M. J. Ryan's book, though, is not to be found at all in Witter Bynner's version, or in any other *Tao Te Ching* version, as far as I have seen. I have not been able to find any older source to it than M. J. Ryan's book. Maybe it is of her invention?

That would be odd, since she used the quote again in The *Happiness Makeover* from 2005, accrediting it to Lao Tzu, but this time she quoted only the first part, which belongs to neither Lao Tzu nor Bynner (page 170). Would she really do that if it were of her own invention?

The accreditation confusion increases. *The Fatigue Prescription* from 2010, by Linda Hawes Clever, uses the complete form of the quote, ascribing it all to Lao Tzu with Witter Bynner as translator (pages 21-22). She has probably picked that up from the Internet, since Ryan never specified the translator.

On the copyright page accreditations Witter Bynner's book is specified as the source to the whole quote, but a 1986 edition instead of the original from 1944. I checked that edition without finding more than the lines in chapter 47 quoted above. In the bibliography she actually lists the Bynner book as from 1994 (page 177), which is just a reprint of the 1986 edition.

I don't think that Clever would miss checking the book to which she referred, so she might have gotten it from the web instead. Although she misses the same line from Bynner as Ryan does, it is not likely that she found the quote there, since no book by Ryan is in her bibliography.

On a section in the book for Internet resources, she lists nine quotation websites. Among them is thetao.info (page 176). Unfortunately that website does not exist anymore, but an Internet Archive search shows that it never contained chapter 47 of *Tao Te Ching*. There are several other web pages ascribing the full quote to Bynner, though of course none of them precedes Ryan's book from 1994.

I assume that the quote from Ryan entered the Internet and somewhere along the way was connected to Bynner as a whole, because of the part from his text. For more about Witter Bynner and his version of *Tao Te Ching*, see the chapter "A man with outward courage."

In my searches I found two books that may have inspired M. J. Ryan to the lines that are not from Bynner. One is in the same genre as hers: *The Wisdom of the Self* from 1992, by Paul Ferrini. He wrote (page 32):

No one else has the answer. No one else is more together. No one else has knowledge that you do not have.

He goes on to state: "Whatever is in Lao Tzu, or Buddha, or Jesus is in you." It is pure speculation, but this may have connected the lines to Lao Tzu in Ryan's mind. Ferrini also wrote a lyrical book inspired by *Tao Te Ching* in form and content: *Virtues of the Way* from 1990. It does not contain the quote examined here, or any parts of it. Nor is Ferrini mentioned in Ryan's book.

The other book that might have inspired Ryan is quite different from Ferrini's and Ryan's, if not to say their antidote: *Coping with Cults* from 1990, by Maryann Miller. This is how she ends the chapter on how not to get in a cult, which is also the last chapter of the book (page 127):

It is so important to remember that no one else has the answer to your problems. All of us have to find our own answers, and it is not as impossible as it seems. The key is to take and keep control of your own life. Don't give it away to anyone.

Well, Miller is also not mentioned in Ryan's book, but like Ferrini's book it was published just a few years before. Of course, what is stated in these three books is nothing exceptional to come out of human minds. It is hardly necessary to link it to Lao Tzu. In short, the message is: Nobody but you can get you what you want. Lao Tzu would not subscribe to it.

Be careful what you water your dreams

"Be careful what you water your dreams with. Water them with worry and fear and you will produce weeds that choke the life from your dream. Water them with optimism and solutions and you will cultivate success. Always be on the lookout for ways to turn a problem into an opportunity for success. Always be on the lookout for ways to nurture your dream."

The first thing that disturbs me with this quote – probably because I am a writer by profession – is the grammar of the first sentence. Should it not be "Be careful with what you water your dreams"? But that sentence only gets a fraction of the results, and several of those have an even more awkward reading: "Be careful with what you water your dreams with."

As for the content, Lao Tzu did not discuss dreams even once in *Tao Te Ching*. Nor did he express himself in this blabbering way, full of nonsensical concepts and metaphors. It is plain ridiculous.

How to nurture one's dreams? By living, of course. But there is no straight relation between one's life while awake and one's dreams. However we choose to live, we get dreams covering the full spectrum, and almost all of them are forgotten long before waking up.

The quote might make a little more sense if by "dreams" wishes and ambitions are intended. If so, why not use these words instead?

Still, terms unfamiliar to Lao Tzu and his time remain – such as optimism and opportunity. These are concepts of our time, the era of getting ahead in life, no matter what. Personal success was to Lao Tzu and his contemporaries the opposite of the Way, which meant that we should all try our best to benefit everyone and everything, not just our own ambitions. Those who cared mainly about their own success were abominable in the eyes of Lao Tzu. Chapter 53 makes it clear what he thought about those who used their powers to enrich themselves (my version):

When the palace is magnificent,
The fields are filled with weeds,
And the granaries are empty.
Some have lavish garments,
Carry sharp swords,
And feast on food and drink.
They possess more than they can spend.
This is called the vanity of robbers.
It is certainly not the Way.

The ideal behavior was that of the sage who understood to give priority to the needs of others. Chapter 7 states:

The sage puts himself last and becomes the first,
Neglects himself and is preserved.
Is it not because he is unselfish that he fulfills himself?

I have not seen the quote examined here, or anything similar to it, in any version of *Tao Te Ching* – and I did not expect it. The oldest books I have found to contain the quote are from 2008, both accrediting it to Lao Tzu without giving a source: *More Than a Mountain: One Woman's Everest* by T. A. Loeffler has the complete quote in the beginning of the book, whereas *Reality check* by Guy Kawasaki has the first two sentences of it (page 366). According to Amazon, Loeffler's book was published April 8, and Kawasaki's October 30, so it is possible that the latter got the quote from the former. But it is more likely that they both got the quote from the Internet.

A Google search finds the oldest posting of the complete quote in a blog from February 8, 2008, ascribing it to Lao Tzu. No later than the same month it appeared on the Goodreads website, where it has by now (August 2020) received almost 1,200 likes, the first of which is from February 9, 2008. That is one day later than the above mentioned blog post, but it is still most probable that Goodreads published the quote first – also that both Loeffler and Kawasaki got it there. On Facebook, it started to appear in 2010, and soon multiplied.

It is strange that this long quote would appear without any trace of its origin, or an explanation to why it was accredited to Lao Tzu to begin with. Still, I could not find a plausible source to it.

The expression "water your dreams" is odd, but not unique to the quote examined here. The oldest occurrence of it I have found is in the book *Can you stand to be blessed?* from 1994, by T. D. Jakes, who is the bishop of a non-denominational church in Dallas. His words are more somber than the quote discussed here (page 167):

> *No one can water your dreams but you. No matter how many people hold your hand, you still must shed your own tears. Others can cry with you, but they can't cry for you! That's the bad news. The good news is there will be a harvest at the end of your tears!*

Next decade, another book with a Christian theme used the same expression with a different tone – *Journey to significance* from 2003, by the pastor Tony Miller (page 167):

No one will ever water your dreams as well as you do! For those who are satisfied to walk in mediocrity, the highway of life has always been paved with good intentions.

There is an earlier book with the expression, even using it as a header for a paragraph: *Breakthrough Secrets: To Live Your Dreams* from 2000, edited by Susan A. Friedmann (page 90). But that short text deals with actual and not metaphorical water, and how essential it is to the body (page 90):

Your body needs water to access its energy potential. Your body's water-powered energy is a serious key to pursuing and manifesting your life's dream. Water is the pathway in which all body functions flow. The body is composed of at least two-thirds water and is critical for every single body function. Your life potential can be evaluated by the water content in your cells. It's evident that we live on a cellular level.

There are similarities between the Christian quotes and the one examined here, but far from enough to decide one of them to be its origin. What can be stated, though, is that nothing in *Tao Te Ching* can be considered the origin.

Be content with what you have

"Be content with what you have; rejoice in the way things are. When you realize there is nothing lacking, the whole world belongs to you."

I have no problem with the first sentence of this quote, and neither would Lao Tzu. Chapter 80 of *Tao Te Ching* describes his ideal world and it is indeed a place where people are at peace with what they have and "rejoice in their daily life," even to the point that they don't ever feel the need to leave their habitat (my version):

> *They can see their neighbors.*
> *Roosters and dogs can be heard from there.*
> *Still, they will age and die*
> *Without visiting one another.*

Also, Lao Tzu would be fine with "there is nothing lacking" – but not with "the whole world belongs to you." The world definitely does not belong to anyone. That would be absurd. We inhabit the world, but none of us owns it. Instead, Lao Tzu insisted that we should be humble about our place in it. If we would try to control it, we would risk breaking it.

He said in chapter 29:

> *Conquering the world and changing it,*
> *I do not think it can succeed.*

The world is a sacred vessel that cannot be changed.
He who changes it will destroy it.
He who seizes it will lose it.

And in chapter 48:

Never take over the world to tamper with it.
Those who want to tamper with it
Are not fit to take over the world.

Lao Tzu was very clear about the world being ruled by *Tao*, the Way, and no one or nothing else. For people to fit in, they needed to follow the Way. Otherwise they were headed for utter failure.

He was not the only one in ancient China to reject the idea of someone taking possession of the world. I dare say that all the thinkers of that era would have agreed wholeheartedly. The world was not something on which any human being could make a claim.

That hubris belongs to our time, and costs both us and the world dearly. In past eras, the earth was regarded as a place for human beings to find their places, not something to conquer. None would even dream it could be done.

In spite of the above, the quote examined here is from a version of *Tao Te Ching*, the very popular one by Stephen Mitchell from 1988. It is the end of chapter 44. As often with Mitchell, his wording deviates quite a lot from other versions. Here is mine:

Those who are content suffer no disgrace.
Those who know when to halt are unharmed.
They last long.

Here is that of James Legge from 1891. He put it in verse, as he did with the rhyming parts of Lao Tzu's text (page 88):

Who is content
Needs fear no shame.
Who knows to stop
Incurs no blame.
From danger free
Long live shall he.

And here is that of Lin Yutang in 1948 (page 218):

The contented man meets no disgrace;
Who knows when to stop runs into no danger —
He can long endure.

Nothing about owning the world, of course. Apart from that, though, Mitchell's version is in agreement with the others. Lao Tzu's message with these lines is that those who know to avoid excess will also avoid a lot of problems.

For more about Stephen Mitchell and his version of *Tao Te Ching*, see the chapter "A good traveler has no fixed plans."

Because of a great love

"Because of a great love, one is courageous."

Lao Tzu was not interested in discussing love. The word appears only twice in my version of *Tao Te Ching*, and in none of the instances is it great. In chapter 13 Lao Tzu speaks of the need to care for the world as much as for oneself, if trusted to rule it (my version):

> *He who loves his body as much as the world*
> *Can be entrusted with the world.*

And chapter 17 lists rulers according to how their subjects regard them:

> *The supreme rulers are hardly known by their subjects.*
> *The lesser are loved and praised.*
> *The even lesser are feared.*
> *The least are despised.*

Nor did Lao Tzu care much for courage. In chapter 73 he even warns about its hazard:

> *Those who have the courage to dare will perish.*
> *Those who have the courage not to dare will live.*

He made no other mention of courage in *Tao Te Ching*. I have not found the quote examined here in any other version of *Tao Te Ching*. The oldest book I have come across with the exact quote is *A Thousand Paths to Love* from 2001, by David Baird (page 216). It is a collection of advice and quotes, where this one is accredited to Lao Tzu, without any source for it.

Another book with the same theme is *1001 Ways to Be Romantic* by Gregory J. P. Godek. Its first edition was published in 1991, and contained advice but no quotes. Quotes were introduced in later expanded editions. In the edition from the year 2000 (section 486, page 157) is a quote stated to be from *Tao Te Ching*:

> *When male and female combine, all things achieve harmony.*

It is from Stephen Mitchell's version of *Tao Te Ching*, chapter 42 (page 42). As usual, Mitchell has given himself some liberty with the text. For more about Stephen Mitchell and his version of *Tao Te Ching*, see the chapter "A good traveler has no fixed plans."

My version of the same lines reads:

> *All things carry yin and embrace yang.*
> *They reach harmony by blending with the vital breath.*

The vital breath is *ch'i* (Pinyin spelling *qi*), the Chinese life energy concept. The ancient Chinese polarity of *yin* and *yang* could also be applied to female and male qualities, but that was definitely not the major thing and not an adequate description of it.

In the 2010 edition of Godek's book, the love and courage quote discussed here was added to the section, accredited to Lao Tzu instead of *Tao Te Ching*. So he might very well have picked it up from Baird's 2001 book. It is not from

Stephen Mitchell's book. And it has nothing to do with Lao Tzu.

Because one believes in oneself

"Because one believes in oneself, one doesn't try to convince others. Because one is content with oneself, one doesn't need others' approval. Because one accepts oneself, the whole world accepts him or her."

The perspective of these lines is self-oriented. It's all about how splendid it is to be pleased with oneself. That is definitely not something Lao Tzu would say or applaud. To him, it was not at all about praising oneself – quite the opposite. His ideal was modesty and humility. For example, in chapter 2 he stated that the sage never demands honor for his deed, adding (my version):

Because he demands no honor,
He will never be dishonored.

And in chapter 7:

The sage puts himself last and becomes the first,
Neglects himself and is preserved.
Is it not because he is unselfish that he fulfills himself?

Again about the sage, in chapter 22:

He does not show off, therefore he shines.
He does not justify himself, therefore he is revered.
He does not boast, therefore he is honored.
He does not praise himself, therefore he remains.

Chapter 63 explains that because the sage does not strive for greatness, he can accomplish it, and chapter 77 says that the sage acts without taking credit, accomplishing without dwelling on it.

The oldest book I have found with the complete quote examined here is *Comfortable in Your Own Skin* from as late as 2014, by Leandie du Randt. The following year there were three books published with the quote. They all ascribed it to Lao Tzu.

The quote appeared several years earlier on the Internet. The oldest occurrence would be on the Goodreads website, where the quote, accredited to Lao Tzu, got its first like on December 19, 2009. On Facebook, the first appearance was in May 2011, also naming Lao Tzu as the author.

So, it is safe to say that the quote in this wording had its origin on the web.

There is a text with similar wording and content to be found on the Internet, but not in any book:

When you believe in yourself, you don't try to convince others. Because you are content with yourself, you don't need others' approval. When you accept yourself, the whole world accepts you also.

It is not ascribed to Lao Tzu – or to anyone else, as far as I have found. But the similarities with the quote examined here are striking. It is not unlikely that they have the same source, which then has been paraphrased in different directions. I don't know what that source is, but it is not Lao Tzu.

Being deeply loved by someone

"Being deeply loved by someone gives you strength, while loving someone deeply gives you courage."

Love is not a subject that Lao Tzu explored in his *Tao Te Ching*. Already that makes it certain: This is a fake Lao Tzu quote.

And if that would not suffice, the clumsy pop song lyrics of the quote are far below what Lao Tzu mustered. Loving deeply – as if there is a meaningful way of measuring it. And if it were measurable, why do it vertically downwards? Might the expression hint at love being profound when it reaches all the way down to the groin?

Furthermore, is strength really what you get from being loved? Not joy, for example? And it may take some courage to express one's love towards somebody, but is that the sole reward of it? The quote kind of implies, involuntarily, that the true blessings come from a love less deep.

In any case, it has nothing to do with what Lao Tzu discussed. Nor would that strange egotistical focus on the sentiment we call love appeal to his contemporaries. This quote has no place in ancient China. It is a modern wording of modern ideas.

The oldest book with the quote I have found is *Lightning* from 1988, by the famous novelist Dean Koontz (at the start of part 1, page 1), using a semicolon instead of a comma after "strength," which is a bit excessive. He accredited it to Lao Tzu, giving no source.

The literary form of the quote has similarities to that of *Tao Te Ching*, but definitely not the content. So, I wonder where Koontz can have gotten it. Even if he was paraphrasing, which is not unlikely with a novelist, he must have done so from another source than Lao Tzu.

The quote is very popular, no doubt partly due to its appearance in Koontz's novel. On the Goodreads website, this is by far the most liked quote ascribed to Lao Tzu, with well over 30,000 likes (August 2020). That is six times more than the second most popular one. It's a pity that this web sensation has nothing to do with Lao Tzu.

Can you step back from your own mind

"Can you step back from your own mind and thus understand all things?"

Step back from your own mind? Only by decapitation. Understand without your mind? Not even in your dreams. I am not fond of quasi-philosophical statements of this kind. They aim to sound profound, but really say nothing.

If "mind" is replaced by, for example, "prejudice" or "misconceptions" there is something intelligible said, and probably Lao Tzu would agree on it. Our minds are full of presuppositions that we need to reexamine, but that would be impossible without the mind.

Lao Tzu's text is partly hard to comprehend, for sure, but it would be unfair to accuse him of being intentionally cryptic. He enjoyed the paradoxes and seemingly impenetrable mysteries of the world, and made no secret of it. But *Tao Te Ching* is mainly celebrated for its clarity and directness. As he said in chapter 70 (my version):

My words are very easy to understand.

The quote examined here aspires to be paradoxical, as if that would make it more profound. Lao Tzu would frown at that.

Surprisingly, this quote is from a version of *Tao Te Ching* — that of Stephen Mitchell from 1988. It is by far the most popular of all English renditions of Lao Tzu's text, though Mitchell has allowed himself quite some liberties in the wordings, often landing far away from the standard translations. Here, too.

The quote is from chapter 10. Here is my version of the same lines:

Can you comprehend everything in the four directions
And still do nothing?

And here is Arthur Waley's wording from 1934 (page 153):

Can your mind penetrate every corner of the land, but you yourself never interfere?

Comprehending and penetrating everything is really the opposite of stepping back from one's mind. Mitchell might have thought of his words as an expression of distancing oneself in order to get the full view.

But there is still a difference between understanding all things and doing nothing or not interfering. Lao Tzu's challenge of sorts is to remain inactive although you have all the answers – actually just because you have the answers, if they are the right ones.

Also with the lines right above these in chapter 10, Mitchell is far away from the usual wordings:

Can you deal with the most vital matters
by letting events take their course?

Here is my version of that part:

Can you open and close the gate of Heaven
And act like a woman?

And Waley's:

Can you in opening and shutting the heavenly gates
play always the female part?

To Lao Tzu, what he regarded as the female characteristic was gentle yielding. This was his ideal, and also how he understood *Tao* to be. He wrote in chapter 6, calling *Tao* the valley spirit (my version):

The valley spirit never dies.
It is called the mystical female.
The entrance to the mystical female
Is called the root of Heaven and Earth.

Human beings should follow that ideal in their behavior. He stated it again in chapter 28:

Knowing the manly, but clinging to the womanly,
You become the valley of the world.
Being the valley of the world,
Eternal virtue will never desert you,
And you become like a little child anew.

It is odd that Mitchell should miss pointing this very significant aspect of Lao Tzu's teaching out in chapter 10. He did not omit it in chapters 6 and 28. For the rest of chapter 10, Mitchell stayed within the translating norm.

For more about Stephen Mitchell and his version of *Tao Te Ching*, see the chapter "A good traveler has no fixed plans."

Care about what other people think

"Care about what other people think and you will always be their prisoner."

These are not Lao Tzu's words, but he would not be completely opposed to them. Not that he would ever consider adapting to what other people might expect of him, or change his views to conform to theirs, but he was saddened by the alienation he felt from just about everyone else.

His solace was his conviction that he understood something they did not, and it was the most important of all – the Way that ruled the world.

Chapter 20 of *Tao Te Ching* differs from the other 80 in its personal tone and melancholy sentiment. He described his isolation from others, who did not understand him, with words approaching anguish. But at the end, he rejoiced at exactly what set him apart – the insight he was given by being aware of *Tao*, which he here called "the great mother."

Here is the end of that chapter (my version), giving a rare glimpse of the man behind the text:

The common people see clearly,
I alone am held in the dark.
The common people are sharp,
Only I am clumsy,
Like drifting on the waves of the sea,
Without direction.

Other people are occupied,
I alone am unwilling, like the outcast.
I alone am different from the others,
Because I am nourished by the great mother.

As for the fake Lao Tzu quote discussed in this chapter, the earliest example of it I have found is in the book *A Million Little Pieces* from 2003, by James Frey (page 180). The book is about his struggle with addiction. He found Lao Tzu's text uplifting and eye-opening.

It is clear in the text that Frey allowed himself to paraphrase, and he did so to make the reader follow his thought process and revelations. We get to experience what he did upon reading the *Tao Te Ching*. And he even mentioned what chapters he referred to, as he went through them. That is far too often ignored in books quoting Lao Tzu. In the second edition, published the following year in Oprah's Book Club, he added this text in the beginning of the book:

The author is particularly grateful to the Chinese classic Tao Te Ching by Lao-Tzu, who is believed to have lived in the 6th century BC. I have read many translations of this ancient text, but Stephen Mitchell's, published by HarperCollins in 1988, is by far the best. I have made a few minor changes in the passages I've quoted with Stephen Mitchell's permission.

I would not agree with his choice, but there it is.

The quote discussed here, Frey relates to chapter 9 of *Tao Te Ching*. In Stephen Mitchell's version, it reads:

Care about people's approval
and you will be their prisoner.

As so often with Mitchell, the wording is a bit odd or even off, compared to other translations. Here is mine:

*Displaying riches and titles with pride
Brings about one's downfall.*

Wing-tsit Chan in 1963 expressed it (page 115):

*To be proud with honor and wealth
Is to cause one's own downfall.*

Philip J. Ivanhoe in 2002 wrote (page 9):

*To be haughty when wealth and honor come your way is
to bring disaster upon yourself.*

I really don't understand how Mitchell came up with his version, omitting the reference to wealth. Was he reluctant to talk ill of the rich and mighty? Furthermore, the thing with being prisoner has no basis in the chapter. Mitchell seems to have replaced the lines with something he preferred to state, regardless of Lao Tzu.

As for the rest of chapter 9, Mitchell's version stays rather close to the original. For more about Stephen Mitchell and his version of *Tao Te Ching*, see the chapter "A good traveler has no fixed plans."

Countless words count less

"Countless words count less than the silent balance between yin and yang."

The wordplay with 'countless' and 'count less' would probably have been appreciated by Lao Tzu, who used little tricks of that kind through *Tao Te Ching*. It even starts by one, playing on the fact that *Tao* can be both a noun and a verb: "The Tao that can be 'Taoed' is not the eternal Tao," which I translated:

The Way that can be walked is not the eternal Way.

I am sure the Chinese readers of it through the millennia were amused. He did it again the following line with 'name' and 'named.'

Also, Lao Tzu was indeed familiar with the concept of the opposing duo *yin* and *yang*. He mentioned them only once by these terms, in chapter 42, but indeed recognized their importance:

All things carry yin and embrace yang.
They reach harmony by blending with the vital breath.

What I translated as "the vital breath" is the ancient idea of life energy, called *ch'i* (*qi* in Pinyin).

Lao Tzu would also agree that that any number of words is less important than silently resting in the balance between *yin* and *yang*, or anything else for that matter. He was not a fan of words, although he wrote just above 5,000 in *Tao Te Ching*. In chapter 5 he stated:

A multitude of words is tiresome,
Unlike remaining centered.

James Legge in 1891 wrote for the same lines, using rhyme in accordance with those lines in the Chinese text:

Much speech to swift exhaustion lead we see;
Your inner being guard, and keep it free.

The Chinese word I translated as 'centered' can also be translated as 'middle' and is used in the name of China. Here it means that Lao Tzu warned against being confused by a multitude of fine words and rhetoric. You should hold fast to your own mind and trust its judgment. It really has nothing to do with *yin* and *yang*.

Still, these are the very lines from which this quote comes, as they are worded in *The Tao Te Ching: A New Translation with Commentary* from 2002, by the musician and acupuncturist Ralph Alan Dale (1920-2006). It is his interpretation of the last lines of chapter 5 (page 10 in the 2016 edition of his book).

Dale allowed himself a lot of freedom with the text. The original does not mention *yin* and *yang* at all in the chapter, and the last line deals with what we would call personal integrity. But to him the whole chapter was about *yin* and *yang*. He started it:

Yin and yang aren't sentimental.
They exist without moralizing.
They act regardless of our wishes

within the ebb and flow
of every pregnant moment.

My version of the same lines reads:

Heaven and Earth are not kind.
They regard all things as offerings.
The sage is not kind.
He regards people as offerings.

Dale ignored that the second set of lines deals with the sage, but his replacement of Heaven and Earth is less offensive. They were traditionally seen as sort of ultimate examples of the polarity, where Heaven was *yang* and Earth was *yin*.

But that polarity was so much more in Chinese tradition – in short *yin* and *yang* were characteristics and not entities of their own. And Lao Tzu did not use the words in chapter 5, but two other opposites of dignity in Chinese thought – well, in traditions all over the world. Heaven and Earth have always in themselves been regarded as fundamental components of the world. Lao Tzu mentioned the pair several times in *Tao Te Ching*.

He did so once more in chapter 5:

Is not the space between Heaven and Earth like a bellows?
It is empty, but lacks nothing.
The more it moves, the more comes out of it.

Dale insisted on *yin* and *yang* there, too:

The space between yin and yang
is like a bellows –

empty, yet infinitely full.
The more it yields,
The more it fills.

Thereby he missed the clever use of the bellows metaphor. It is easy to picture the dynamic space between Heaven and Earth, and how the movements in it create a multitude. But between *yin* and *yang* – what kind of space is that, and how can it fill by yielding?

It is as if Dale wanted to replace *Tao* with *yin* and *yang* as the fundamental principle of the world. Lao Tzu would not have that.

Dale used the word *Tao* in his version, for example in the beginning of chapter 1, mentioned above. But in the same chapter he introduced the concept "the Great Integrity" and used it in many other chapters where Lao Tzu wrote *Tao*.

It is a confusing choice, making the Way even more cryptic than it already is. Or as Lao Tzu stated in the line of chapter 5 discussed here: "A multitude of words is tiresome."

Ralph Alan Dale's version of *Tao Te Ching* is also discussed in the chapter "If you are depressed."

Do you imagine the universe is agitated?

"Do you imagine the universe is agitated? Go into the desert at night and look at the stars. This practice should answer the question."

It is a safe bet that the stars don't care what we do or think. But in ancient times the heavenly objects and their movements were regarded as very much connected to earthly life. Out of that rose astrology. Also, heaven was regarded as the domain of deities, who kept a close watch on human behavior – and it frequently got them agitated.

The overall perspective in the distant past was geocentric, placing earth in the middle of it all. And people knew by storms, eclipses, comets, and other heavenly phenomena, that the sky was full of dramatic events, which were mysterious and therefore all the more threatening. The indifference of the universe with its billions of stars is a recent concept, introduced by the advances of astronomy.

Lao Tzu spoke repeatedly about heaven in *Tao Te Ching*, often describing its workings as *T'ien Tao*, Heaven's Way. And Heaven's Way was not limited to events in the sky, but could be experienced everywhere on earth as well. Chapter 47 states (my version):

> *Without looking through the window,*
> *You can see Heaven's Way.*

So, to Lao Tzu there would be no point in walking into the desert to look at the stars.

Mostly, he paired Heaven and Earth as sort of the framework of everything in the world. In chapter 25 he presented a hierarchy of sorts:

Man is ruled by Earth.
Earth is ruled by Heaven.
Heaven is ruled by the Way.
The Way is ruled by itself.

To him, as to most ancient thinkers in China and elsewhere, it was all connected.

The quote examined here must be of modern making, and it is: *Hua Hu Ching: The Unknown Teachings of Lao Tzu* from 1992, interpreted by Brian Browne Walker (chapter 5, page 7). *Hua Hu Ching* is a text falsely claimed to be by Lao Tzu, and Walker's version of it is a very free rendering of an also very free rendering by Hua-Ching Ni from 1979.

After the words of the quote, Walker continued the chapter:

The superior person settles her mind as the universe settles the stars in the sky. By connecting her mind with the subtle origin, she calms it. Once calmed, it naturally expands, and ultimately her mind becomes as vast and immeasurable as the night sky.

Ni's corresponding part of chapter 5 reads:

The mind can be just as immeasurable as the universe itself. An integral being settles his mind just as the vast universe settles itself. He unites his mind with the unnameable Subtle Origin and its expression as the mul-

tiuniverse in which there is no past, present or future.
This is how an integral being deals with his mind.

None is even remotely similar to anything in *Tao Te Ching*.

For more on *Hua Hu Ching*, see my chapter "Embrace all things."

Doing nothing is better

"Doing nothing is better than being busy doing nothing."

Doing nothing is something very familiar to Lao Tzu, indeed. It is his concept of non-action, *wu-wei*, which he mentioned a lot in his *Tao Te Ching*. The sage knows to do as little as possible and thereby the most is accomplished, at least the most beneficial.

Also being busy doing nothing can, though by a stretch, be connected to his thoughts. But what he meant was rather that trying to do a lot accomplishes nothing. He saw no effort in doing nothing, so how could someone be busy with it?

The oldest source I have found to this quote is a book from 1950: *Explorations in Altruistic Love and Behavior*, edited by the sociologist Pitirim Sorokin. In one of the book's essays, by Sorokin and D. S. Gove, they write (page 298):

> ... Laotse's old wisdom that the best government is that which governs least, that doing nothing is better than being busy doing nothing, and that the more various punitive laws are enacted the more numerous become the criminals.

Their wording clearly indicates that they are paraphrasing *Tao Te Ching*. The last statement is undoubtedly from chapter 57, where the relevant lines read (my version):

The more laws and commands there are,
The more thieves and robbers there will be.

As for the principle of governing with as little action as possible, Lao Tzu mentions it several times in his text, also in chapter 57:

Use non-action to govern the world.

But there is no comparison of doing nothing as opposed to being busy doing nothing in that chapter – or any other one.

Sorokin must still have grown attached to this strange paraphrasing of Lao Tzu's principle. He used it in another essay from the same year, published in the book *Sociometry in France and the United States*, edited by Georges Gurvitch (page 219), where he called it a "Taoist dictum," not mentioning Lao Tzu. And again in his own book *The ways and power of love* from 1954 (page 369), claiming it to be both a Taoist and Buddhist statement.

Embrace all things

"Embrace all things as part of the Harmonious Oneness, and then you will begin to perceive it."

If this is to be regarded as a Taoist saying, the "Harmonious Oneness" can be nothing but *Tao*, the Way, The expression is rather pompous and elaborate, but not completely off. *Tao* is definitely the one, in Lao Tzu's world, but it is modest and yielding, and that is not the spirit of this expression.

Lao Tzu simply called it "the one," but he did talk about embracing it – for example in chapter 10 (my version):

Can you make your soul embrace the one
And not lose it?

And in chapter 22:

Therefore, the sage embraces the one,
And is an example to the world.

But he would insist that if you manage to embrace it, you do more than just begin to perceive it – you grasp and accept it. When *Tao* is perceived it is comprehended, and there is no scale to that. You see it or you don't. Once you do, you are there.

So, the quote examined here is not from *Tao Te Ching*, although it is not all that far away. It is from another Taoist text: *Hua Hu Ching: The Unknown Teachings of Lao Tzu* from

1992, interpreted by Brian Browne Walker (chapter 48, page 59 in the 1995 paperback edition).

Hua Hu Ching is a text claimed to be by Lao Tzu, but it is probably not older than the 4th century CE, at least 700 years after the time of Lao Tzu. Except for fragments found among the Dunhuang manuscripts discovered in 1900, it does not exist in a complete trustworthy form from historical times. The title means "Classic on Converting the Barbarians," because it was written to discredit Buddhism. It was even accompanied by the claim that Lao Tzu had gone to India after leaving China, and introduced thoughts that were later developed into Buddhism.

A complete version of *Hua Hu Ching* in 81 chapters (like *Tao Te Ching*) was written by Hua-Ching Ni, first published in 1979: *The Complete Works of Lao Tzu: Tao Teh Ching and Hua Hu Ching*. As the title suggests, it also contains his version of *Tao Te Ching*. About his version of *Hua Hu Ching* he stated (page 105): "This one is my own education from my parents. The writing is my personal attainment." The style and content of the text are far away from the raw agitation in the fragments from Dunhuang.

As for Brian Browne Walker's version of *Hua Hu Ching*, he mentioned with affection in the introduction that he was indebted to Hua-Ching Ni and his version of the same text. But Walker put it in poetic form, similar to *Tao Te Ching*, whereas Ni's version is in prose. Walker's expression "Harmonious Oneness" is in Ni's version either "Universal Way" or "Universal One." These and other differences make the texts so far apart, it is hard to see that they can be interpretations of the same classic. And of course, they are not.

The chapter in question describes two paths to spiritual cultivation – one affirmative and one by denial. The quote discussed here ends the explanation of the first path. In Walker's version it reads:

The first is the path of acceptance.
Affirm everyone and everything.
Freely extend your goodwill and virtue in every direction, regardless of circumstances.
Embrace all things as part of the Harmonious Oneness, and then you will begin to perceive it.

This is Ni's version (pages 162-163):

One is the affirmative approach which accepts and includes everything with a positive attitude. From an ethical point of view, it means extending universal virtue to all, regardless of any external condition. This is different from the relative, affirmative attitude that is expounded by religions and which includes some things or people and excludes others. According to the Universal Way, the affirmative approach excludes nothing.

These differences might be the reason for Ni's 1995 edition of his book having this statement on the copyright page:

The material in this book is more than a translation, it is an elucidation drawing upon Hua-Ching Ni's decades of spiritual cultivation and training in the tradition in which these works originated. Anyone who wishes to produce their own version of this material should work directly from an original text rather than copying from Hua-Ching Ni's work.

He says almost exactly the same thing on page 107. I have not been able to check if the 1979 edition contains the same words.

His advice would not be easy to follow, since there is no complete original text of *Hua Hu Ching*. In any case, neither Walker nor Ni can be said to quote Lao Tzu – not by a long shot.

Quotes from *Hua Hu Ching* are also discussed in these chapters: "Do you imagine the universe is agitated," "Highly evolved people," "If you want to awaken all of humanity," and "Most of the world's religions."

Emptiness appears barren

"Emptiness appears barren, yet is infinite fullness."

This is a strange saying. The first part would work just as well reversed: barrenness appears empty. Of course, emptiness does not have the exact same meaning as barrenness. The former is an absolute, where the latter is somewhat relative – it can mean that something is missing, but something else is there. So, if the former is intended, the barren of the saying must be replaced by something as absolute, like void or for that matter empty. What is said is really just that emptiness appears empty.

The problem with 'infinite fullness' is similar. If it's full, it's full, otherwise not full. Adding "infinite" makes no difference. The word implies that the fullness goes beyond the space it fills, and that would just be expanding that space endlessly – like our universe, which is anything but empty. Whatever space is intended in the quote, it's either full or not full of whatever is filling it. Finite fullness would make more sense, or just fullness. Thus, for example: Emptiness appears empty, yet is full.

Yes, full of emptiness, in the sense that there is no part of it that is not empty.

The quote is not really something that Lao Tzu would claim. He enjoyed wordplay and paradoxes, but was also careful to make statements clarifying that he was indeed talking about something, not just nothing. Still, this is from a version of *Tao Te Ching* – that by A. J. Girling from 2015 (copyright 2014). It is from chapter 45.

To make sense of it when compared to other versions, it is necessary to reflect on the first few lines of that chapter. Girling's version reads (page 61):

The seemingly defective
lacks no perfection
Emptiness appears barren
Yet is infinite fullness

Here is my version of the same lines:

The most complete seems lacking.
Yet in use it is not exhausted.
The most abundant seems empty.
Yet in use it is not drained.

D. C. Lau in 1963 had this wording (page 106):

Great perfection seems chipped,
Yet use will not wear it out;
Great fullness seems empty,
Yet use will not drain it.

So, it's not that emptiness feels barren, but that the full seems empty. And the point is that still, it can't be drained. Also, it is not that the seemingly defective lacks no perfection, but the most perfect seems lacking. Yet, it is not exhausted.

That full and perfect thing of which Lao Tzu spoke is *Tao*, the Way. To him, it was the driving principle of the whole world, and although as hard to see as if hidden, it never stopped and never failed. Lao Tzu more than once used the paradox of this the mightiest force seeming the vaguest. For example, chapter 4 states (my version):

The Way is empty, yet inexhaustible,
Like an abyss!

And chapter 6:

Though gossamer,
As if barely existing,
It is used but never spent.

And chapter 37:

The Way is ever without action,
Yet nothing is left undone.

Girling might have been a bit eager to find a unique wording. On Amazon, the author is introduced by these words: "A J Girling was introduced to Taoism, and initiated by a Taoist Master, in the 1980's. Since then Girling has dedicated extensive time to the research and contemplation that resulted in the translation of this edition of the Tao Te Ching."

The Taoist Master's name is not mentioned, nor anything about Girling's own background, academic or other.

The bibliography in Girling's book contains 25 *Tao Te Ching* versions (pages 123-125), esteemed ones as well as some less trustworthy. Still, checking through the interpretations of some of the other chapters, I wonder with what intention the author has consulted all those versions.

The same year as the above mentioned book, Girling released *Tao Te Ching: with Comparative Quotes from Aristotle to Zhuangzi*, which has more than twice the number of pages. I would be surprised if this were not the first manuscript. In it, each chapter of *Tao Te Ching* is followed by Girling's comments and quotes from a wide variety of thinkers. That is a splendid idea, provided that the versions of the *Tao Te Ching* chapters are trustworthy. I have my doubts about that.

Every human being's essential nature

"Every human being's essential nature is perfect and faultless, but after years of immersion in the world we easily forget our roots and take on a counterfeit nature."

This long quote is far from the style of Lao Tzu. Its content also deviates considerably from what is expressed in *Tao Te Ching*. Still, it is not impossible to see connections to Taoist philosophy in it.

It is doubtful that Lao Tzu would call every human being's essential nature perfect, but he was certain that nature itself was. To him, everything in the world was governed by the same faultless principle of *Tao*, the Way. So, we would all do fine if we just conform to it. The impression Lao Tzu gave is that only humans are able to deviate from *Tao* – and it is not to our advantage.

Forgetting our roots can be interpreted as another expression of what Lao Tzu stated frequently in his text: so many of us have lost connection to *Tao* and that leads us far astray. If what we thereby have is a counterfeit nature, though, makes less sense. How can it be counterfeit if it is from ignorance? What we have forgotten leads us astray, but that cannot be a conscious effort. The problem is ignorance, maybe even folly, but not pretense.

The earliest example of this exact quote I have found is in the self-improvement book *Excuses Begone! How to Change Lifelong, Self-Defeating Thinking Habits* from 2009, by Wayne W. Dyer (1940-2015), a prominent writer in that field. It is accredited to Lao Tzu without specifying the source (at the start of part I, page 1).

I have not found the quote in any version of *Tao Te Ching*, not even in Dyer's previous books on the Taoism theme, where he went through all the 81 chapters and commented them: *Change Your Thoughts – Change Your Life: Living the Wisdom of the Tao* from 2007, and the 2008 version called *Living the Wisdom of the Tao: The Complete Tao Te Ching and Affirmations*.

Dyer readily admitted to being inspired by *Tao Te Ching*, quoting and commenting it frequently in several of his books. In *Excuses Begone!* he started the introduction (page xi): "I spent the year 2006 immersed in the ancient teachings of Lao-tzu, studying his monumental tome, the Tao Te Ching."

His many quotes from Lao Tzu's text were his own interpretations, often getting quite far from the original. In *Change Your Thoughts — Change Your Life* he explained acquiring ten versions of *Tao Te Ching*, listed in the acknowledgments: "From those ten translations I'd gone over, I pieced together the 81 passages in Change Your Thoughts — Change Your Life, based on how they resonated with me" (page xii). In *Living the Wisdom of the Tao*, published the following year, that had grown to "pieced together after reviewing hundreds of translations" (page 1). Still, his acknowledgements contain only the same ten books (page 167).

He used some of the translations more than others. In 2010, Stephen Mitchell filed a lawsuit against him for copyright infringement of 200 lines from Mitchell's version. It was settled out of court the following year.

I have noticed that many of Dyer's *Tao Te Ching* wordings are identical with those of Mitchell. That can happen when translating a text of this kind, since it contains only about 5,000 words and uses a limited set of concepts repeatedly. Still, I have found it surprisingly rare in other books. And Mitchell's case is different, since he often deviated considerably from the standard translations. In those cases, Dyer's use of the same words was particularly compromising.

It was also kind of alarming that Dyer did not mention his particular dependence on Mitchell's version, since he was happy to do that courtesy with another source in *Living the Wisdom of the Tao* (page 3): "Some versions of the Tao I relied upon more than others, and I would like to especially mention that the version provided by Jonathan Star (in *Tao Te Ching: the Definitive Edition*) was the one I quoted most extensively and the one that most resonated with my vision and interpretation of the Tao."

Both Mitchell's and Star's book are mentioned in his list of ten *Tao Te Ching* versions mentioned above. The list is significant in lacking any of the prominent old translations, such as those of James Legge from 1891, Arthur Waley from 1934, and D. C. Lau from 1963. The only exception might be that of the French Jesuit and sinologist Léon Wieger from 1913, but it is an English 1999 translation by Derek Bryce of the French original.

Anyway, as far as I have found – searching Google as well as Facebook – Dyer is the origin of the quote examined here, and it seems that he allowed himself to find his own wording for what he regarded as Lao Tzu's message. But then he should not really have put the wording between quotation marks.

Other debatable Dyer Lao Tzu quotes are discussed later in this book. See the chapters "If a person seems wicked," "New beginnings," "When you find the way," and "Your own positive future."

Figure out the rhythm of life

"Figure out the rhythm of life and live in harmony with it."

This would make sense coming out of the mouth of someone like Miles Davis. There may be something like a rhythm of life and if there is, Miles Davis would probably have gotten it. He would have said: "Just play it!" We are born with a bang and then rush to follow the beat, which seems to accelerate by each year, until it all suddenly stops. Then there is silence.

Harmony, too, is a concept familiar to any musician. Rhythm and harmony are not necessarily connected in music, but surely they are both enforced if joined.

Still, the perspective is not that of Lao Tzu. He never mentioned rhythm, and when he spoke about harmony he referred to the pleasant state of balance and peace by accepting what is natural. The sage knows it, according to chapter 49 (my version):

The sage is one with the world,
And lives in harmony with it.

I have not been able to find the origin of the quote examined here. It seems to have appeared during the 2010's, frequently attributed to Lao Tzu, and is mainly spread by memes. On the Goodreads website it has been present since at least July, 2012, which was when it got its first like.

The only book in which I have found the quote is the Kindle ebook *Laozi: His Words* from 2014, by Daniel Coenn. It is only 23 pages and most likely just a collection of quotes accredited to Lao Tzu found on the Internet. This one is not the only quote in the book falsely ascribed to Lao Tzu.

But there are books making similar statements, also within the literature on Taoism, such as *An Illustrated Introduction to Taoism: The Wisdom of the Sages* from 2010, by Jean C. Cooper (1905-1999). It contains her book from 1972, *Taoism: The Way of the Mystic,* and some additional essays of hers. The introduction says about Taoism (page 1):

> *It is the philosophy of the rhythm of life and simplicity of mind and spirit together with the absence of calculated activity, as expressed in the doctrine of wu-wei, and the presence of spontaneity, balance, and harmony.*

This sentence might have been paraphrased into the quote examined here. But of course, it is not a translation of anything from Lao Tzu.

The expression "rhythm of life" is also used within Christian literature, where it signifies the time we have on earth, from birth to death, and how to do the best of it. For more on that, see my chapter "There is a time to live," which deals with a quote somewhat similar to the one discussed here.

From wonder into wonder

"From wonder into wonder existence opens."

Existence would be a strange word in the mouth of Lao Tzu. He used an ancient expression, the ten thousand things, which meant the whole world and everything in it. Existence implies the opposite of non-existence, and what would that be? Lao Tzu had no interest in something illusionary. He talked about reality as he saw it, and the conditions to which it was bound.

Wonder, on the other hand, is an expression he could relate to. He found so much in the workings of the world amazing, especially what he saw as everything's root: *Tao*, the Way. He frequently praised it in *Tao Te Ching*, calling it "the origin of all things" and yet it modestly "becomes one with the dust" (chapter 4, my version).

In spite of the above, the quote examined here is actually from an interpretation of *Tao Te Ching*: the book *The Way of Life According to Laotzu* from 1944, by Witter Bynner. He called it "An American Version." The quote is from the end of chapter 1, but Bynner's version is quite distant from other translations.

In these lines, the relation between what Bynner calls the core and the surface is explained (page 25):

The core and the surface
Are essentially the same,
Words making them seem different

Only to express appearance.
If name be needed, wonder names them both:
From wonder into wonder
Existence opens.

Bynner's choice of "core" and "surface" is an interesting alternative to the usual translations. The former refers to *Tao*, the Way, and the latter to how it is expressed in the world. The chapter explains that you need to be free of desires to observe the former and full of desire to observe the latter.

I used "mystery" and "manifestations" for those two aspects of reality (earlier in the chapter). Here is my version of the same last lines:

These two have the same origin but differ in name.
That is the secret,
The secret of secrets,
The gate to all mysteries.

Arthur Waley in 1934 used "Secret Essences" and "Outcomes," ending the chapter (page 141):

These two things issued from the same mould, but nevertheless are different in name.
This 'same mould' we can but call the Mystery,
Or rather the 'Darker than any Mystery',
The Doorway whence issued all Secret Essences.

D. C. Lau in 1963 used "its secrets" and "its manifestations," where "it" is *Tao*. His ending of the chapter reads (page 57):

Being the same they are called mysteries,
Mystery upon mystery –
The gateway of the manifold secrets.

The complication with Bynner's version is the word "existence," especially since that was the term he used for *Tao* throughout his translation. It is a strange choice. According to Lao Tzu, *Tao* is the cause and ruler of existence, but not the same as it. How could something cause and rule itself?

What mystery or secret the gate opens to is indeed something unclear also after reading the following 80 chapters of *Tao Te Ching*. It might even be the essence of *Tao* – but it is not *Tao* itself, or Lao Tzu would just have used that word again, as he did three times in the opening line of that chapter, which is a play of words that Bynner's solution can't catch. Tao can be both a noun and a verb, so the line says: "The Tao that can be 'Taoed' is not the eternal Tao." In my version:

The Way that can be walked is not the eternal Way.

James Legge in 1891 stayed with not translating *Tao*, but was still able to point out the pun (page 47):

The Tâo that can be trodden is not the enduring and unchanging Tâo.

Bynner's beginning of the chapter misses that little joke:

Existence is beyond the power of words to define.

He should have been more careful with choosing his own words.

For more about Witter Bynner and his version of *Tao Te Ching*, see the chapter "A man with outward courage."

Give evil nothing to oppose

"Give evil nothing to oppose and it will disappear by itself."

Evil is a vague concept. What is evil to one may be benevolent to someone else. Really, what is evil? In Christianity it forms a polarity with its opposite good, like black and white – but among people it is mostly a question of nuances of grey in between the extremes.

An important question arises: are there evil people, or just evil deeds? Just about every action movie is based on the concept that some people are evil to the core, living their lives trying to cause pain and mayhem, as if it were their nutrition.

Aristotle in *Poetics*, his text about the rules of tragedy, claimed that the characters in a story should be defined by the moral standard of their actions, and not some latent urge to do evil or good. Both moral and immoral choices could lead to tragic endings. Furthermore, he demanded that their actions should be forced on them by circumstances, not some free choice. They did what they had to do, or they were unaware of the consequences, and then one thing led to another and so on.

I think that is how we mostly are and act – driven by events out of our control. It is also implied by Christian dogma. Otherwise it could not claim that everyone, no matter what, can be forgiven. In Christianity, only the devil is evil to the core – and even that can be debated. He, too, is believed to be part of God's plan.

Tao Te Ching implies that Lao Tzu had a similar view. He did not talk about evil, but about such things as confusion, emotions, and ignorance. People – and especially their rulers – just needed to discover and follow *Tao*, the Way, and they would all be gentle. Chapter 32 states about the Way (my version):

If princes and kings could follow it,
All things would by themselves abide,
Heaven and Earth would unite
And sweet dew would fall.
People would by themselves find harmony,
Without being commanded.

He was not unaware of people being good or bad, in the sense of doing good or bad things, but he regarded these circumstances as so to speak workable. None should be rejected. Chapter 62 begins:

The Way is the source of all things,
Good people's treasure and bad people's refuge.

Fine words are traded.
Noble deeds gain respect.
But people who are not good,
Why abandon them?

So, the concept of evil as we know it was not relevant to Lao Tzu. Still, the quote discussed here is from a version of *Tao Te Ching* – that by Stephen Mitchell from 1988. It is his wording for the last lines of chapter 60.

In this book I express doubts about his versions of several parts of Lao Tzu's text. Mitchell takes considerable liberties to make Lao Tzu say what he thinks the ancient thinker should. In this case he has gone so far that it makes no sense to compare just the last lines with other versions, so I will use a bigger portion of the chapter for comparison. Here is Mitchell's version (page 60):

> *Center your country in the Tao*
> *and evil will have no power.*
> *Not that it isn't there,*
> *but you'll be able to step out of its way.*
>
> *Give evil nothing to oppose*
> *and it will disappear by itself.*

Here is my version of the same lines:

> *When the world is ruled according to the Way,*
> *The ghosts lose their power.*
> *The ghosts do not really lose their power,*
> *But it is not used to harm people.*
>
> *Not only will their power not harm people,*
> *Nor will the sage harm people.*
> *Since neither of them causes harm,*
> *Unified virtue is restored.*

And here is the version by Wing-tsit Chan from 1963 (page 207):

> *If Tao is employed to rule the empire,*
> *Spiritual beings will lose their supernatural power.*
> *Not that they lose their spiritual power,*
> *But their spiritual power can no longer harm people.*
> *Not only will their supernatural power not harm people,*
> *But the sage also will not harm people.*

When both do not harm each other,
Virtue will be accumulated in both for the benefit (of the people).

Probably, Mitchell wanted to avoid any talk of ghosts or spirits, but replacing it with evil as some kind of entity is quite misleading. Also, it forced him to make other changes, equally misleading. For example, how to step away from evil – isn't that simply fleeing? And he missed the interesting circumstance of the sage not causing harm – implying that in some cases, the sage could.

The ghosts that Lao Tzu spoke of are *kuei*, restless spirits of deceased ancestors. When the land is ruled by *Tao* they have no reason to interfere, but they do not disappear. Occurrences of what we call the supernatural are extremely rare in *Tao Te Ching*. Lao Tzu focused on the real world and real people.

For more about Stephen Mitchell and his version of *Tao Te Ching*, see the chapter "A good traveler has no fixed plans."

He who controls others

"He who controls others may be powerful, but he who has mastered himself is mightier still."

Controlling others is an expression that is out of place in the world of Lao Tzu. He talked about ruling, definitely, but that was something reserved for kings and such. Their rule would improve if they used caution and tried to follow *Tao*, the Way – but mastering themselves would be odd, like a ruler turned slave, albeit by his own command. It would make little sense in ancient China.

Also the idea that there is some measure to the power of the monarch was strange to Lao Tzu and his contemporaries. The emperor had his power, no matter what, and it was quite close to absolute. Lao Tzu would know, since legend has it that he worked at the imperial archives before leaving the country in disgust.

So, the wording of this quote points at later times than ancient China and another mentality than that of Lao Tzu. Still, the quote is not altogether off. There is a similar passage in *Tao Te Ching*.

The quote is from the 1958 book *Tao Teh King by Lao Tzu: Interpreted as Nature and Intelligence*, by the philosophy professor Archie J. Bahm (1907-1996). It is his version of part of chapter 33. Here is the same part in my version:

> *Those who defeat others are strong,*
> *Those who defeat themselves are mighty.*

Other translators have used words like conquer or overcome. The idea of defeating oneself being superior to defeating others is well known – for example in sports, especially the martial arts. Athletes should not strive just to be better than their opponents, but to improve themselves beyond what they perceived was their limit. So, the world record holder should try to surpass even that feat, instead of settling complacently.

Bahm's version might seem close, but his choice of the words "control" and "master" imply suppression rather than improvement. Similar objections can be made about other wordings in Bahm's rendering of this *Tao Te Ching* chapter. Here it is (page 36 in the 1996 edition):

He who knows much about others may be learned, but he who understands himself is more intelligent.
He who controls others may be powerful, but he who has mastered himself is mightier still.
He who receives his happiness from others may be rich, but he whose contentment is self-willed has inexhaustible wealth.
He who occupies a place provided for him by others may live a long life, but he who dwells in his own self-constituted place, even though he decays, is eternal.

Concepts such as intelligence and happiness are strange to Lao Tzu, and the two last sentences deviate in quite an elaborate way from the original. Lao Tzu's writing may be difficult to comprehend, but it was straightforward and void of ornaments. Here is my version of chapter 33:

Those who understand others are clever,
Those who understand themselves are wise.

Those who defeat others are strong,
Those who defeat themselves are mighty.

Those who know when they have enough are rich.
Those who are unswerving have resolve.
Those who stay where they are will endure.
Those who die without being forgotten get longevity.

This *Tao Te Ching* chapter is the most famous for its last line, which in some Chinese manuscripts had wordings seeming to suggest the possibility of eternal life. James Legge in 1891 translated it (page 75):

He who dies and yet does not perish, has longevity.

This led to a Taoist movement trying to find a method by alchemy to achieve immortality. But they got it wrong. Lao Tzu spoke about reputation, and not actual personal survival. You can live on in others' memories, but that's it. This was confirmed by the Mawangdui manuscripts from around 200 BC, discovered in the 1970's.

To Bahm's credit he sort of hinted at the same, although with a bundle of words hard to extract from the original.

For more about Archie J. Bahm's version of *Tao Te Ching*, see the chapters "One who is too insistent" and "Respond intelligently."

A slightly different wording of the quote examined here is also widely spread on the web:

Mastering others requires force;
Mastering the self needs strength.

As stated above, I am not fond of the choice "mastering," which implies suppression rather than improvement, but I object even more to the expression "the self." That is a psychoanalytical concept, also used in Buddhist literature, but it would have been odd to hear from Lao Tzu.

It is from the popular 1972 *Tao Te Ching* version by Gia-fu Feng and Jane English. For more on their version of chapter 33, see "Knowing others," and their quote from Chuang Tzu is discussed in "Life and death are one thread."

Health is the greatest possession

"Health is the greatest possession. Contentment is the greatest treasure. Confidence is the greatest friend. Non-being is the greatest joy."

This might pass as something Lao Tzu would have said, except for the last sentence. Not only was he rather uninterested in joy, but non-being was no ingredient in his cosmology. He did not even show the least interest in what might come after death. And the sage he spoke of in *Tao Te Ching* was definitely being, though far from noisy or intrusive.

Well, Lao Tzu would also be at least ambiguous about confidence, if not specifically in *Tao*, the Way. Otherwise, he would praise humility more. And health was not something he discussed in *Tao Te Ching*.

This quote would be something more in line with Buddhist thought, and indeed, that is where it originated. The earliest example of this quote I have found is in the book *The Dhammapada: the Path of Perfection* from 1973, translated by Juan Mascaró (page 64). The only difference in the wording is "nirvana" instead of "non-being," but that is pretty much the same. It is the Buddhist term for "becoming extinct," in the meaning of exiting the cycle of rebirth, the only way to end suffering.

Dhammapada is a collection of aphorisms on the Buddhist strife for nirvana, from around the third century BC.

The earliest book I have found accrediting the quote to Lao Tzu is *The 6 Sacred Stones* from 2008, a novel by Matthew Reilly (page 257), using "nonbeing" instead of "nirvana." The change of that word indicates an adaption of the quote from a Buddhist origin to something less obviously so. Still, it does not make the quote Taoist.

Matthew Reilly might not be the first one to claim Lao Tzu as the source of the quote. By 2008 (or 2007, when his book was first published in Australia), he could have found web pages giving him that impression. That is something I have not been able to confirm, though.

The oldest Internet appearance of the quote ascribed to Lao Tzu I have found with an ascertained date is from November 2008 in the blog Financial Philosopher. It refers to two sources – D. C. Lau's version of *Tao Te Ching* from 1963 and *The Complete Idiot's Guide to Eastern Philosophy* from 2000, by Jay Stevenson – but the quote is in none of these books. The earliest Facebook posting of the quote ascribed to Lao Tzu is from April 2010, using the Chinese characters for his name. But both before and after that date there are also posts ascribing it to Buddha or *Dhammapada*, albeit with slightly different wordings.

On Goodreads, the quote is also accredited to Lao Tzu, but has only four likes (August 2020), the first one from as late as 2013.

So, it might be that Matthew Riley was the origin of the mistaken accreditation of this quote to Lao Tzu. But it would be strange if he made this error when using *Dhammapada* as his source. It is more likely that he mixed up sources when picking from some list of old quotes that I have not been able to find.

Highly evolved people

"Highly evolved people have their own conscience as pure law."

I don't hesitate to admit that I find this quote, supposedly from Lao Tzu, very objectionable.

Highly evolved people? That's social Darwinism, the repulsive idea that some people are more developed than others, as if natural selection by mutation would create people superior to their own species. It does not work that way. And if people assumed superior would use their own conscience as pure law, it simply means that they claim to be above the law of ordinary men.

My impression of Lao Tzu and his thoughts is that he would object to it just as strongly. Instead he stated repeatedly that those who were sage put themselves below others, like water flows to the lowest places. Modesty and discretion were his ideals, not presumption.

The quote is definitely not from *Tao Te Ching*. Unfortunately the mistaken accreditation of it to Lao Tzu is somewhat supported in a book containing both his words and those of a much later text falsely claiming to transmit his words: the *Hua Hu Ching*, probably composed no earlier than the 4th century CE. The exact quote can be found in *The Complete Works of Lao Tzu: Tao Teh Ching and Hua Hu Ching* from 1979, by Hua-Ching Ni (page 199).

I have serious doubts also about the English wording of this quote, supposedly from *Hua Hu Ching*. Neither "evolved" nor "conscience" are concepts fitting Chinese thinking that far back. Anyway, it has nothing whatsoever to do with Lao Tzu.

For more on *Hua Hu Ching*, see my chapter "Embrace all things."

Hold your male side

"Hold your male side with your female side
Hold your bright side with your dull side
Hold your high side with your low side
Then you will be able to hold the whole world"

This quote, listing three pairs of opposites and saying that balancing them gives you command of the world, points to the Chinese division of *yin* and *yang*. They are the fundamental opposites in ancient Chinese thinking, where the latter represents light and heaven, and the former represents darkness and earth.

The famous symbol of their unity shows both sort of embracing within a circle, but there is a dot of *yin* in *yang* and vice versa. This means that they complement one another to make a whole, and there is always some *yin* in *yang* and some *yang* in *yin*. It is in their combination and balance that they reach perfection.

Lao Tzu was quite familiar with the concept of *yin* and *yang*, regarding it as a fundamental attribute of the world. He stated in chapter 42 of *Tao Te Ching* (my version):

All things carry yin and embrace yang.
They reach harmony by blending with the vital breath.

The vital breath is *ch'i* (spelled *qi* in Pinyin), the Chinese concept of a life energy.

Chapter 42 is the only one where *yin* and *yang* are mentioned, but the idea of balance between opposites is a recurring theme in Lao Tzu's text. The quote here, though, is questionable as an interpretation of his thoughts.

Balancing your male and female sides is both understandable and commendable, but what are your bright and dull sides, or your high and low sides? Most of all, holding the whole world is something Lao Tzu warned against. Chapter 29 of *Tao Te Ching* begins:

> *Conquering the world and changing it,*
> *I do not think it can succeed.*
> *The world is a sacred vessel that cannot be changed.*
> *He who changes it will destroy it.*
> *He who seizes it will lose it.*

The world is best served by being left alone. Its rightful ruler is none but *Tao*, the Way.

Still, the quote examined here is actually from a version of *Tao Te Ching*: Jonathan Star's *Tao Te Ching: The Definitive Edition* from 2001. The book contains his own English version of the text, as well as a Chinese language version of it where every word is explained. The latter is a convenient resource for anyone studying Lao Tzu's text. I used it quite a lot when working on my English version of *Tao Te Ching*.

The quote is the beginning of Star's version of chapter 28. But it deviates considerably from other translations. In my version the same lines read:

> *Knowing the manly, but clinging to the womanly,*
> *You become the valley of the world.*
> *Being the valley of the world,*
> *Eternal virtue will never desert you,*
> *And you become like a little child anew.*

Robert G. Henricks in 1989 wrote (page 242):

When you know the male yet hold on to the female,
You'll be the ravine of the country.
When you're the ravine of the country,
Your constant virtue will not leave.
And when your constant virtue doesn't leave,
You'll return to the state of the infant.

So, Lao Tzu did not balance the male and female – he preferred the female, and of high and low he preferred the low, which is the valley or ravine. Nor did he mention bright and dull, but insisted on *te*, virtue. Instead of holding the world, he said that by the virtue of humbling yourself you will become as innocent as a child.

I can't guess how Star got to his interpretation. There is not much support for it in the Chinese language part of his book.

Another example of Jonathan Star's free interpretation of *Tao Te Ching* can be found in the chapter "If a person seems wicked" of this book.

Hope and fear are both phantoms

"Hope and fear are both phantoms that arise from thinking of the self. When we don't see the self as self, what do we have to fear?"

The self is a concept heavily attired with lots of traits that can differ considerably between for example psychology with Freudian and Jungian roots, and spiritual perspectives of Hinduism and Buddhism. But there is none of that in the Taoism of Lao Tzu. He did not regard the individual as wrestling with some kind of identity issue. Some people were far from *Tao*, the Way, and some were not – and that was it.

People who were unbalanced and agitated were not obsessed by themselves. They were simply caught in aspirations blinding them to what they already had. Chapter 50 states (my version):

> We go from birth to death.
> Three out of ten follow life.
> Three out of ten follow death.
> People who rush from birth to death
> Are also three out of ten.
> Why is that so?
> Because they want to make too much of life.

Hope was not something Lao Tzu discussed. It may have been implicit in some of his comments about the human nature, for example in the lines from chapter 50 above, but he regarded it as wanting rather than hoping. The former expresses an urge, the latter a dream. The one who urges for something believes it is possible to reach, whereas hoping for something implies that it is completely out of one's reach. Hope is what one does when there is nothing else one can do.

He spoke about fear, though. What caused people's fear was their longing for praise and worries about its opposite disgrace. Chapter 13 explains:

Praise leads to weakness.
Getting it causes fear, losing it causes fear.

When you are praised you worry about losing it, so it weakens you. If you were concerned with neither praise nor disgrace, it would not bother you. But the aspiration to get the former makes you fear the latter.

The quote examined here is actually from this chapter of *Tao Te Ching*, in the version by Stephen Mitchell from 1988. As so often in his version, he allowed himself a lot of freedom from the original text.

Here is my version of the same lines:

The reason for great distress is the body.
Without it, what distress could there be?

Arthur Waley in 1934 wrote (page 157):

The only reason that we suffer hurt is that we have bodies; if we had no bodies, how could we suffer?

Nothing about hope or "the self." The lines are instead about the vulnerability of having a body. It is an interesting statement by Lao Tzu, which sort of goes along with the saying "Sticks and stones may break my bones, but words will never hurt me." Were it not for the vulnerability of the physical body, falling out of grace would not be harmful to anything but one's pride.

Stephen Mitchell has gone down another path in his interpretation. I can't see how his wording can be an option if Lao Tzu's text is to be treated with some faithfulness. Mitchell has not translated this chapter (and several others), but taken it as a starting point for saying something belonging much more to his mindset than that of Lao Tzu. I fail to see how that was necessary.

For more about Stephen Mitchell and his version of *Tao Te Ching*, see the chapter "A good traveler has no fixed plans."

If a person seems wicked

"If a person seems wicked,
do not cast him away.
Awaken him with your words,
elevate him with your deeds,
repay his injury with your kindness.
Do not cast him away;
cast away his wickedness."

I might be overly sensitive, but the word wicked strikes me as misplaced in the translation of a philosophical Chinese text from around 2,400 years ago. But the general message in this quote is something Lao Tzu would not deny. Those who are bad should not be condemned and abandoned – they should be converted. He wrote in chapter 27 of *Tao Te Ching* that "the sage takes care of all people, forsaking none" and later in the chapter:

> *So, a good person is the bad person's teacher.*
> *A bad person is the good person's task.*

The quote examined here seems like it could be an elaboration of these lines from chapter 27, but it is not. It originates in the book *Change Your Thoughts, Change Your Life: Living the Wisdom of the Tao* from 2007, by Wayne W. Dyer (page 294), where it is expressly stated in the header to be from chapter 62.

That is confusing, since the chapter in question contains little similar to the quote. Here is the corresponding part of the chapter in my version:

Fine words are traded.
Noble deeds gain respect.
But people who are not good,
Why abandon them?

Bernhard Karlgren in 1975 wrote, for some reason omitting the question mark (page 11):

With fine words one can buy honours, with fine actions one can surpass others. The bad ones among men, why need they be rejected.

Now, in the preface to his book (page xv), Dyer gladly confesses to his dependence on Jonathan Star's *Tao Te Ching: The Definitive Edition* from 2001 for his versions of many *Tao Te Ching* chapters, also specifically chapter 62. He is not just being polite. The same part of chapter 62 reads almost exactly the same in Star's version (page 75). The only difference is that Star wrote "requite" instead of "repay."

Still, Star's version is just as far off from scholarly translations of the lines. It is strange in his case, because later in his book, he gives a word by word translation of the Chinese text, hardly supporting his own interpretation.

Jonathan Star's version of *Tao Te Ching* is also discussed in the chapter "Hold your male side with your female side" of this book. For more about Wayne W. Dyer and his interpretations of *Tao Te Ching*, see the chapter "Every human being's essential nature."

If there is to be peace

"If there is to be peace in the world,
There must be peace in the nations.
If there is to be peace in the nations,
There must be peace in the cities.
If there is to be peace in the cities,
There must be peace between neighbors.
If there is to be peace between neighbors,
There must be peace in the home.
If there is to be peace in the home,
There must be peace in the heart."

This long quote ascribed to Lao Tzu is not to be found in *Tao Te Ching*. But there is something at least similar in form, in chapter 54 (my version):

> *Cultivate virtue in yourself,*
> *And it will be true.*
> *Cultivate virtue in the family,*
> *And it will be overflowing.*
> *Cultivate virtue in the town,*
> *And it will be lasting.*
> *Cultivate virtue in the country,*
> *And it will be abundant.*
> *Cultivate virtue in the world,*
> *And it will be universal.*

Therefore:
See others as yourself.
See families as your family.
See towns as your town.
See countries as your country.
See worlds as your world.

Peace is not synonymous with virtue, but the Chinese term *te*, which I translate as virtue, is a diffuse one. Other versions choose other words for it, though "virtue" is by far the most common translation. Arthur Waley in 1934 called it "power" and James Legge in 1891 translated it "attributes (of the Tao)." But peace would not really be adequate for the word.

The virtue implied is the one of following *Tao*, the Way. That leads to peace, Lao Tzu definitely claimed, but it is far from all. Although unlikely, there could be peace without both *Tao* and *te*. It would be a fragile peace, probably based on oppression by mighty forces. Peace can be very costly and even tormenting. The virtue Lao Tzu spoke of leads to a peace that pleases everyone.

The quote examined here would fit better with the philosophy of Confucius, who insisted on the necessity of the people being loyal to their families all the way up to the ruler. But he, too, is not the source to this quote.

The earliest example of this exact quote I have found is in *Lifeskills* from 1997, by Virginia and Redford Williams (page xix), accrediting it to Lao Tzu with the reservation that it might be from Mo Tzu. No source to this is given.

Mo Tzu is a probable alternative source to the quote, but where Lao Tzu's focus was virtue, Mo Tzu's was love – not peace per se. Still, it would lead to peace. The below quote is from Book 4 of Mo Tzu's work, the last paragraph of the chapter called "Universal Love III," translated by Y.

P. Mei in *The Ethical and Political Works of Motse* from 1929 (page 97):

> *Therefore, universal love is really the way of the sage-kings. It is what gives peace to the rulers and sustenance to the people. The gentleman would do well to understand and practise universal love; then he would be gracious as a ruler, loyal as a minister, affectionate as a father, filial as a son, courteous as an elder brother, and respectful as a younger brother.*

By "gentleman" Mo Tzu meant someone with a quality quite near to what Lao Tzu described as virtue. It is also very similar to what he called "the sage."

Still, neither Lao Tzu nor Mo Tzu is the source to the exact quote examined here, or for that matter anything close enough to it. I have not found its origin, but it is likely to be either a very free paraphrasing of chapter 54 in *Tao Te Ching*, or the words of someone else that were later assumed to be Lao Tzu.

If you are depressed

"If you are depressed, you are living in the past. If you are anxious, you are living in the future. If you are at peace, you are living in the moment."

This fake Lao Tzu quote has also been accredited to Warren Buffet, the billionaire, and to the Brazilian motivational speaker Junia Bretas.

Bretas is quoted in a translation to English with the exact above wording, on the front page of the *West Los Angeles Buddhist Temple Bulletin*, volume 57, July-August 2014.

The Buffet quote has the same wording, but with the following addition: "Past is waste paper, present is newspaper, and future is a question paper!" It seems that Buffet quoted someone else and then added his own metaphor to it. The Buffet reference is from a 2015 book by David Conellias: *Let's Do Life* (page 30). Could it be that Warren Buffet had read the Buddhist bulletin?

The Junia Bretas quote was pointed out in a February 2014 comment to a blog post about the quote. Maybe the writer of the Buddhist bulletin had read that when publishing the quote with Bretas as its originator.

Her text in Portuguese, though, seems not to be exactly the same as the quote, as far as I can judge from Google Translate. Here are her words, if you happen to read Portuguese: "Depressão é excesso de passado em nossas mentes. Ansiedade excesso de futuro. O momento presente é a chave para a cura de todos oa males mentais."

It is close to the fake Lao Tzu quote, but not spot on. Especially in the last sentence they differ considerably. Google Translate gives "The present moment is the key to the cure of all mental evils," and it seems to be a decently accurate translation. That's quite far from "If you are at peace you are living in the moment."

So, it is possible that there is another source to the fake Lao Tzu quote than Junia Bretas.

It is surely not Lao Tzu. Depression and anxiety are modern concepts, alien to ancient China. Not only that. The idea of living in the past, the future, or the present would make no sense to Lao Tzu and his contemporaries.

If anything, he preferred the past, which is something he mentioned more than once in his book. He would flat out deny the possibility of living in the future. That's something modern society invented. And the idea of living in the now is more Zen than Taoism.

But then there is a book accrediting the quote to a *Tao Te Ching* version by the musician and acupuncturist Ralph Alan Dale (1920-2006), which was published in 2002. This quote is in *On the Journey: The Art of Living with Breast Cancer*, by Cynthia Thomas, 2014 (page 30).

Dale's version of *Tao Te Ching* deviates from the norm, to say the least. He called *Tao* "the Great Integrity," which is hard to find reason for in any understanding of the Chinese concept. But I can't find the quote examined here in the editions of his *Tao Te Ching* translation that are accessible on the Internet.

Either he is misquoted by Cynthia Thomas, or there were edits made in later editions of his book. Anyway, it has stopped me from figuring out what lines of *Tao Te Ching* he might have interpreted that way – if he ever did so. If Dale wrote those lines at all, he might have done so in a comment to Lao Tzu's text, and not as a translation of it.

Ralph Alan Dale's version of *Tao Te Ching* is also discussed in the chapter "Countless words count less."

The mystery intrigued me to spend quite some time searching the Internet. The earliest occurrence of the quote I found in Google searches was on the Goodreads website, where the quote is accredited to Lao Tzu and got its first like on March 21, 2012. Next was a blog post from April 12, 2012, also accrediting Lao Tzu. It was picked up in a social anxiety forum on May 22 the same year, stating a Facebook posting from "a few months ago" as its source to the quote.

To my surprise, I got further back on a Facebook search. The first appearance of the quote on Facebook, already accrediting it to Lao Tzu, is from December 19, 2009. It was posted by a girl a few days before she turned 20. It got two likes. The following year, there were more than a dozen posts with the quote – most of them not naming Lao Tzu as the source. The year after that, 2011, there was a flood of them, many mentioning Lao Tzu.

A similar statement was posted on Facebook on June 30, 2009, without giving a source: "When I am anxious it is because I am living in the future. When I am depressed it is because I am living in the past."

That in turn led me to the book *Words of Wisdom* from 2006, written by Rev. Run, a minister with a TV show. This is on page 31, without reference to any source:

> *LIVE IN THE NOW! When I am anxious, it is because I am living in the future. When I am depressed, it is because I am living in the past. We crucify ourselves between two thieves: regret for yesterday and fear of tomorrow.*

I have a feeling that Rev. Run might be the origin of the quote, later transformed and claimed to be Lao Tzu's.

My guess is also that Rev. Run got it from somewhere, but I have failed to discover where.

Another fake Lao Tzu quote with similar meaning is also discussed in this book: "There is a time to live and a time to die, but never to reject the moment."

If you do not change direction

"If you do not change direction, you may end up where you are heading."

Accrediting this quote to Lao Tzu is insulting to his intellect. It is pure nonsense in a presumptuous form. If you don't change direction, where else would you end up but where you are heading?

Actually, the quote makes a mistake in tenses. Even if you change direction, you end up where you *are* heading, but not where you *were* heading before changing direction.

So, double nonsense.

Lao Tzu was not much for travel. His main objection to it was that you find no higher truth elsewhere than right where you are. If it's not there, it is nowhere. In chapter 47 he stated (my version):

Without stepping out the door,
You can know the world.
Without looking through the window,
You can see Heaven's Way.
The longer you travel, the less you know.

And in chapter 80, where he described his ideal society, people should not be inclined to travel:

Although they have boats and carriages,
There's no occasion to use them.

So, for Lao Tzu it was not about taking a trip where you allow yourself to end up just about anywhere. It was about being at peace where you are and remaining there.

The oldest book I have found with this exact quote is *The Dragon Doesn't Live Here Anymore: Loving Fully, Living Freely*, by Alan Cohen, from 1981 (page 355). Already there, Lao Tzu is accredited with it – without any source, to no surprise. Cohen is a successful writer of so-called inspirational books.

Among his many books is one called *The Tao Made Easy* from 2018. There, the excerpts from *Tao Te Ching* he used are from the Gia-fu Feng and Jane English version in the 2011 edition. The quote discussed here, though, is not to be found in their book.

The same quote, just replacing "may" with "will," is found in several books, most of them calling it a Chinese proverb. None of them is older than that of Cohen. So, they may have gotten it from his book, and paraphrased it.

If you realize that all things change

"If you realize that all things change, there is nothing you will try to hold on to. If you are not afraid of dying, there is nothing you cannot achieve."

This fake Lao Tzu quote is easily found on the Internet, though sometimes just the first sentence.

All things changing is really a Buddhist concept. Even more so is the idea of not holding on. Especially in Zen, letting go is praised as a way towards emptiness of the mind. Lao Tzu would describe it differently.

Lao Tzu did speak about the fear of dying, for example when in chapter 74 saying that people without that fear were hard to rule. But overcoming the fear was not something he discussed, and certainly not for the intent of achieving things. He preached *wu-wei*, non-action, which is pretty much the opposite to boldly start doing stuff.

Therefore, it is disappointing to see that the quote is indeed from a version of *Tao Te Ching*. It's in chapter 74, mentioned above, of Stephen Mitchell's popular book from 1988 (page 74). Mitchell has allowed himself considerable freedom in his interpretations of Lao Tzu, frequently leading far away from the mind of the ancient Chinese thinker.

Here is my version of the same lines in chapter 74 of *Tao Te Ching*:

If people are not afraid of dying,
Why threaten them with death?
If people live in constant fear of death,

And if breaking the law is punished by death,
Then who would dare?

That is quite different from the meaning suggested by Mitchell's wording. Every scholarly translation I have come across shows the same distance to Mitchell's version. For example, here is the elegant wording of Victor H. Mair from 1990 (page 49):

If the people never fear death,
what is the purpose of threatening to kill them?
If the people ever fear death,
and I were to capture and kill those who are devious,
who would dare to be so?

In these lines, Lao Tzu discussed politics in a manner not so very far from that of Machiavelli in *The Prince*. A ruler who wants to keep his subjects in check should consider what threats might work. Not very compassionate, but in Lao Tzu's time the authority of the ruler was not to be questioned – even Lao Tzu insisted on it, though himself often critical.

By the way, I have to object to Lao Tzu's conclusion here. Already in his day it must have been obvious that the capital punishment was no guarantee against crime.

The next half of the chapter makes a much more interesting observation. Here is my rendering of it:

There is one appointed supreme executioner.
Truly, trying to take the place of the supreme executioner
Is like trying to carve wood like a master carpenter.
Of those who try to carve wood like a master carpenter,
There are few who do not injure their hands.

This is much easier to agree with. Lao Tzu points out that no executioner can compare to the very master: nature. It is the fact that we will all die, whatever we do. So, society should hesitate to play with death. It can backfire in so many ways. Indeed, history has proven it again and again.

Instead of execution, Mitchell's version speaks of "trying to control the future." Don't ask me where he got that from. Maybe he wanted to avoid the grim subject, and Lao Tzu's mixed treatment of it.

For more about Stephen Mitchell and his version of *Tao Te Ching*, see the chapter "A good traveler has no fixed plans."

If you want to awaken all of humanity

"If you want to awaken all of humanity, then awaken all of yourself. If you want to eliminate the suffering in the world, then eliminate all that is dark and negative in yourself. Truly, the greatest gift you have to give is that of your own self-transformation."

One of the memes with this quote depicts what seems to be a Buddhist monk, which makes sense since the message of the fake Lao Tzu quote relates to Buddhist ideas. Buddhism was not introduced in China until hundreds of years after the time of Lao Tzu.

Awakening oneself and the suffering in the world are familiar concepts in Buddhism, but not in the Taoism of Lao Tzu. Self-transformation is a modern concept with connections to Buddhist as well as other schools of thought. It is close to the self-realization ideas of contemporary society. I'm not sure that even Buddha would have ascribed to it just like that, and surely not Lao Tzu.

Nor would Lao Tzu talk about what is dark and negative within a person, as if a shadow possessed the mind. He spoke about actions, not personality, and insisted that all people should be able to learn to follow *Tao*, the Way – not for what it did to their minds, but for what it would do to their lives and to the world around them.

The quote comes from chapter 75 (page 96) of a 1992 version of *Hua Hu Ching*, a book falsely claiming to contain the words of Lao Tzu. For more about that book, see the chapter "Embrace all things." Unfortunately, this version of the book, by Brian Browne Walker, repeats the false claim. But the *Hua Hu Ching* was written many centuries after Lao Tzu, and it contains ideas at least as far from those of Lao Tzu as the ones mentioned above.

Actually, Walker's rendition of *Hua Hu Ching* is also very far from the original of that book, which exists only in fragments. He has used a version equally far from the original, if not to say fictional, by Hua-Ching Ni from 1979. Walker's version deviates considerably from that book, as well. For example, chapter 75 is to Walker a poetic one-page rendition, but in Ni's book it is several pages of prose (pages 217-220).

The false Lao Tzu quote is also widely spread in the shorter form of just the last sentence:

> *Truly, the greatest gift you have to give is that of your own self-transformation.*

If you want to become whole

"If you want to become whole,
let yourself be partial.
If you want to become straight,
let yourself be crooked.
If you want to become full,
let yourself be empty.
If you want to be reborn,
let yourself die.
If you want to be given everything,
give everything up."

I would be fine with this saying as one by Lao Tzu, were it not for that thing about dying to be reborn. He showed no belief in such a thing. That is Buddhism and Hinduism, not Taoism.

Yet, this is from a version of *Tao Te Ching* – that of Stephen Mitchell from 1988. His very popular text is the origin of many odd Lao Tzu quotes floating around. Mitchell allowed himself a lot of paraphrasing, to say the least. In several instances he landed so far from the original that it can be difficult to figure out what part of *Tao Te Ching* he interpreted and what could make him deviate so far from it.

The quote discussed here is Mitchell's version of the first lines of chapter 22. Of course, it says nothing about rebirth. Here is my version of the same lines:

Hulk to be whole.
Bend to be straight.
Empty to be filled.
Wear down to be renewed.
Reduce to gain.
Excess confuses.

Here is Arthur Waley's wording from 1934 (page 171):

To remain whole, be twisted!
To become straight, let yourself be bent.
To become full, be hollow.
Be tattered, that you may be renewed.
Those that have little, may get more,
Those that have much, are but perplexed.

Obviously, it is the thing about being renewed that Mitchell has taken very far, indeed. I have no idea why. Did he want to turn Lao Tzu into a Buddhist?

For more about Stephen Mitchell and his version of *Tao Te Ching*, see the chapter "A good traveler has no fixed plans."

If you would take

"If you would take, you must first give. This is the beginning of intelligence."

This Lao Tzu quote is gravely misleading. I would not call it intelligent to give in order to take back. Who would accept it? Nor is it gentle and compassionate, as Lao Tzu insisted we should be.

Furthermore, the word "intelligence" is not really fitting on a text from ancient China. Although the word has a long history, its present meaning is from 20th century psychology and the dubious idea that something fundamentally important about the human mind's capacity can be decided by a written test using mathematical and other riddles. Lao Tzu did instead regard people as able, though not always willing. Chapter 53 of *Tao Te Ching* states (my version):

> *The great Way is very straight,*
> *But people prefer to deviate.*

He even warned against confidence in intellectual prowess. Chapter 19 starts:

> *Abandon wisdom, discard knowledge,*
> *And people will benefit a hundredfold.*

Sadly, the quote examined here is from a *Tao Te Ching* version, and by a sinologist at that: Lionel Giles (1875-1958), whose father was also a distinguished sinologist. It is his version of lines from chapter 36 in *The Sayings of Lao Tzu* from 1904 (page 45). In his defense, the quote is taken out of context, which makes it seem to state something else than it does.

Here is the whole beginning of the chapter in his version – and notice also that the last sentence has a slightly different wording than the quote examined here:

If you would contract, you must first expand. If you would weaken, you must first strengthen. If you would overthrow, you must first raise up. If you would take, you must first give. This is called the dawn of intelligence.

The listing of opposites presupposing one another broadens the perspective, but I must still say that Giles has made a rather aggressive interpretation, as if Lao Tzu were talking about winning a battle. And one important line is missing at the end, which is because Giles divided the text of *Tao Te Ching* into themes, cutting and shuffling chapters accordingly.

Here is my version of that part of chapter 36, including the missing last line, which makes all the difference in the world:

What should be shrunken must first be stretched.
What should be weakened must first be strengthened.
What should be abolished must first be cherished.
What should be deprived must first be enriched.
This is called understanding the hidden.
The soft and weak overcome the hard and strong.

Here is D. C. Lau's 1963 wording of the last line (page 95):

The submissive and weak will overcome the hard and strong.

Lao Tzu did not cherish might and force. Nor was he with these words giving a strategy for some conquest. He implied that the enhanced states were vulnerable, because they could be reversed. What is not stretched can't be shrunken, and so on. Moderation is the key.

Still, there is some connection to the subject of warfare. The chapter ends (my version):

The fish cannot leave the deep waters.
The state's weaponry should not be displayed.

A display of force may not only worry one's own people, but it also tends to instigate war. One should not flaunt what powers one has. That makes others want to challenge them.

In conclusion, I cannot really call this Lao Tzu quote fake. The deception lies in what is excluded from it.

Kindness in words

"Kindness in words creates confidence. Kindness in thinking creates profoundness. Kindness in giving creates love."

Any Lao Tzu quote containing the word love is almost certainly fake. That's something he did not discuss in *Tao Te Ching*.

How we emphasize and understand love is something that has evolved through two thousand years of Christianity. Not that the sentiment was unknown to thinkers of antiquity around the world, but it was presented differently, and overall much less so. Lao Tzu didn't dwell on it at all.

Also kindness is something that would make Lao Tzu wonder. He spoke about *te*, which can be translated as virtue, noble actions of a noble mind. That would be a kind way of behaving – mostly but not necessarily. He stated rather ominously in chapter 5 (my version):

Heaven and Earth are not kind.
They regard all things as offerings.
The sage is not kind.
He regards people as offerings.

Although Lao Tzu was evidently compassionate, his text talks about principles extracted from an order that is the one of nature itself. Kindness is not really the thing. Modesty would be something he related to with much more comfort – humility and modesty.

Profoundness is an awkward word in English. Should it not rather be profundity? At least it would be more elegant when translating a philosophical text more than two thousand years old. But the quote has nothing to do with Lao Tzu, if it's not from a very off translation of his text. There are many such translations.

Amusingly, there are also Internet sites and memes accrediting the quote to Mao Zedong, the former Chinese leader. I wouldn't think he had that much to say about love, either.

I have also found the quote accredited to the Greek fabulist Aesop, in *Scientific Concepts Behind Happiness, Kindness, and Empathy in Contemporary Society* from 2019, edited by Nava R. Silton (page xxv). Unfortunately, there is no source specified. Also some websites claim Aesop as the origin of the quote, but this may simply be a misreading of collections, where quotes of Aesop and Lao Tzu are listed one after the other. There are many of those.

According to a learned blog discussion on the Useless Tree website (uselesstree.typepad.com) in August 2008, the earliest appearance of the quote in an English language book is *Peter's Quotations: Ideas for Our Time*, by Laurence J. Peter, 1977. He is most famous for *The Peter Principle*.

Peter claimed it to be a quote from Lao Tzu (page 279), but gave no source to that claim, nor the number of a *Tao Te Ching* chapter.

There is one more quote accredited to Lao Tzu in Peter's book (page 292): "The greater the number of laws and enactments, the more thieves and robbers there will be." This quote originates in *The Sayings of Lao Tzu* by Lionel Giles (page 38), which is from 1904 but with many later editions. Giles translated *Tao Te Ching*, but rearranged the chapters according to topics.

Peter's quote about kindness, though, is not from this

source. It is likely that he got it from a book published the year before, in 1976: *Living thoughts: Inspiration, Insight, and Wisdom from Sources throughout the Ages*, by Bernard S. Raskas. It has the kindness quote on page 143, accrediting it to Lao Tzu.

If I have to guess, I'd say that this fake quote is an off interpretation of a few lines in chapter 67 of *Tao Te Ching*. Here is my version of them:

By compassion one can be brave.
By moderation one can be generous.
By not claiming to be first in the world one can rule.

Another possibility is that the quote is a distorted version of a few lines from chapter 8:

A good mind is deep.
A good gift is kind.
A good word is sincere.

But that's a stretch.

Knowing others

"Knowing others is wisdom, knowing yourself is enlightenment."

A less spread variation of this quote has "the self" instead of "yourself," which is even less likely to originate with Lao Tzu than the one discussed here. The self is a concept used in psychology and sometimes in modern interpretations of Buddhist thought, but it would be alien to the ancient China of Lao Tzu.

So would, of course, the term enlightenment, which is connected to Buddhism – and to the philosophical revolution of 18th century Europe. So, this quote is in neither form from Lao Tzu.

Sadly, though, it is from a version of *Tao Te Ching*, and in its less fortunate form, using "the self." The quote is the beginning of chapter 33 in the Gia-fu Feng and Jane English translation from 1972, which is still in print and quite popular after all these years. The first half of the chapter reads (the book lacks pagination):

Knowing others is wisdom;
Knowing the self is enlightenment.
Mastering others requires force;
Mastering the self needs strength.

The third and fourth line often appear on the web as a separate Lao Tzu quote. With a slightly different wording, it is discussed in the chapter "He who controls others" of this book.

Here is my version of the beginning of chapter 33:

Those who understand others are clever,
Those who understand themselves are wise.
Those who defeat others are strong,
Those who defeat themselves are mighty.

Here is James Legge's wording from 1891 (page 75):

He who knows other men is discerning; he who knows himself is intelligent. He who overcomes others is strong; he who overcomes himself is mighty.

I can't say I like Legge's use of the word "intelligent," which is odd in a text from ancient China. But that is not the issue at hand. Also, I have far more objections to the expressions "the self" and "enlightenment" in the Feng and English version. They make Lao Tzu more of a Buddhist than a Taoist.

It saddens me to find this shortcoming in their version, since it was the first *Tao Te Ching* book I ever got, back in 1973, and it got me started on my lifelong fascination with Lao Tzu's text.

So, it is kind of a relief that they have been slightly misquoted in most later renditions, replacing "the self" with "yourself" at both instances. Replacing "enlightenment," though, is not that common. Since the most accurate replacement is "wisdom," that word would need to be replaced with something else in the first line, or the quote becomes nonsensical.

Victor H. Mair in 1990 also used "enlightenment" but avoided "the self" (page 100):

Understanding others is knowledge,
Understanding oneself is enlightenment.

Arthur Waley in 1934 found a clever solution (page 184):

To understand others is to have knowledge;
To understand oneself is to be illumined.

Illumined is, of course, a synonym to enlightened, but without its Buddhist connotation.

For more on the Feng and English version of chapter 33 see "He who controls others." Also, a quote of theirs from Chuang Tzu is discussed in "Life and death are one thread."

Another version of the quote discussed here, which is also found a lot in books and on the web, is that of Stephen Mitchell's *Tao Te Ching* from 1988 (page 33):

Knowing others is intelligence;
knowing yourself is true wisdom.

Like Legge, he made use of the rather non-archaic word intelligence, the modern use of which is most prominent in psychology – and not without being questioned, especially its application in IQ-testing. Contrary to Legge, though, Mitchell used it in the first instead of the second line. That makes sense, since the word wisdom gives the impression of surpassing intelligence, and thereby the lines come very close to Lao Tzu's intention.

For more about Stephen Mitchell and his version of *Tao Te Ching*, see the chapter "A good traveler has no fixed plans."

Knowledge is a treasure

"Knowledge is a treasure, but practice is the key to it."

Lao Tzu was no friend of knowledge, at least not in the sense of hoarding it and striving to be learned. He stated bluntly in chapter 19 of *Tao Te Ching* (my version):

Abandon knowledge and your worries are over.

To him, the great truth about how the world works was not to be found by learning a lot, but by opening one's mind to it. In chapter 48 he wrote:

Those who seek knowledge,
Collect something every day.
Those who seek the Way,
Let go of something every day.

As for treasures, Lao Tzu had three, none of them being knowledge. He listed them in chapter 67:

I have three treasures that I cherish.
The first is compassion.
The second is moderation.
The third is not claiming to be first in the world.

But there was one more treasure of his, surpassing all the others – *Tao*, the Way. Chapter 62 starts:

The Way is the source of all things,
Good people's treasure and bad people's refuge.

Finally, regarding practice, Lao Tzu was hesitant, to say the least, about its value. He insisted on *wu-wei*, the principle of non-action. The less you need to do, the better. The more you do, the higher the risk that things go wrong. The supreme example of this was *Tao*. He wrote in chapter 37:

The Way is ever without action,
Yet nothing is left undone.

So, the quote discussed here cannot be from Lao Tzu.

In books and on the Internet, he is not the only one frequently being accredited to it. Also, the British physician Thomas Fuller (1654-1734) has received that honor, and in his case it is deserved. The quote is from his big collection of 6,496 proverbs *Gnomologia* from 1732.

It is proverb 3139, with the only difference being that nouns are written with capital initials, according to the custom of the time (page 134, mistakenly marked as 132):

Knowledge is a Treasure, but Practice is the Key to it.

Another proverb on the same page has a similar meaning. It is number 3137:

Knowledge directeth Practice; but yet Practice increaseth Knowledge.

By the way, there is a proverb in his collection to which Lao Tzu might be much more favorable. It is number 4901 (page 212):

There is much more Learning than Knowledge in the World.

This implies wisdom rather than knowledge, and links to Lao Tzu's idea of the sage. It is not about what you learn, but what you understand.

The proverb from Fuller's collection has not only been ascribed to Lao Tzu. *Encyclopaedia of Indian Proverbs*, volume 4, from 1960, by Narasingha Rao, obviously claims it is Indian (page 50). *A Dictionary of American Proverbs* from 1996, edited by Mieder, Kingsbury and Harder, found it in Illinois, New York and Ontario (page 354). *The Magic* from 2012, by Rhonda Byrne, ascribed it to the Arabian 14th century scholar Ibn Khaldun (page 17).

The earliest books I have found accrediting the quote to Lao Tzu are from as late as 2016, and there are three of them. That means they probably got the quote from the Internet.

There, the oldest web page with an ascertained date, accrediting the quote to Lao Tzu, is on Goodreads, where it got its first like on March 20, 2008, just one year after the website was launched. Next was a blog post from May 24, 2010. The blog is Chinese, but lists a number of Lao Tzu quotes in English – also the complete *Tao Te Ching* in Chinese.

That might not have spread considerably over the web, at least not in the West, but I also found a PDF on the web, published in October 2012: *The Amazing Quotes of Lao Tzu*, complied by Remez Sasson. That one might have reached a wider audience, but was probably compiled from the web.

On Facebook, the quote started to appear in 2010, very scarcely. In 2013 it was accredited to Thomas Fuller in a post. The first post ascribing the quote to Lao Tzu came in September of 2015, accompanied by a meme. It was by the author and healer Deborah King, getting 642 likes and 262 shares. So, I presume that's when the linking of the quote to Lao Tzu really took off.

Leadership

"Leadership is your ability to hide your panic from others."

Connecting this quote to Lao Tzu seems like a joke. That is fitting, since the saying is humorous to begin with. One would hope that competent leadership has other qualities than restrained panic. Both "leadership" and "panic" are concepts that relate to our zeitgeist, but hardly the era of Lao Tzu.

Regarding leaders, he talked about princes and kings, not just any kind of boss. And he would revolt against the idea that their primary talent would be the ability to hide their panic. Such a leader would not get Lao Tzu's approval.

He expected much more of them – primarily the understanding of *Tao*, the Way, and what that meant to a ruler. In short: not to act more than absolutely necessary and not demand to get credit for what one accomplished. Humility should be their primary characteristic. Chapter 39 of *Tao Te Ching* says (my version):

> *The noble must make humility his root.*
> *The high must make the low its base.*
> *That is why princes and kings call themselves orphaned, desolate, unworthy.*
> *Is that not to make humility their root?*

Panic would lead to desperate measures, the worst possible scenario in Lao Tzu's view.

The oldest source to this exact quote I have found is from the Australian magazine *Aircraft & Aerospace – Asia Pacific* from the year 2000 (page 58). There the quote is accredited to the Australian rugby coach Jack Gibson. Him as the origin makes much more sense than Lao Tzu, who surely could not even imagine a sport like that.

A slight variation of the quote can be found in a book five years older, *The Key to Great Leadership* from 1995, by the Canadian tennis coach Peter Burwash (page 124):

> *I recently read a great definition of leadership which said, "It's the ability to hide your panic from others."*

Unfortunately, Burwash did not mention where he read it. Perhaps Jack Gibson had read this book or the unspecified source to the quote.

The oldest book with a slight variation to the quote in a Google book search is *NHS Factivities: Facts and Activity News from the Natural History Survey* from 1986, writing "the others" instead of just "others." It seems to be in a list of anonymous quotes, but I have not been able to examine the book.

There is a book from 2004, which might explain how the quote got ascribed to Lao Tzu: *Financially Speaking* by Robert A. Leo (page 45). It ends with "everyone" instead of "others," and states the source to be anonymous. But the quote right after that one is from Lao Tzu – "To lead the people, walk behind them" (from chapter 66 of *Tao Te Ching*). So, others may have mixed it up when repeating the quote examined here.

I have the impression that this is true for several fake Lao Tzu quotes circling around. Accreditations have been mixed up.

The earliest ascertained example of the quote I have

found on the Internet is on a gymnastics forum, in a comment from January 19, 2008, ascribing it to an anonymous source. The quote returns on several other websites the following years, also marking its origin as anonymous.

The first time Lao Tzu is accredited on the web, as far as I have found, is in 2014. Richard Branson, the founder of Virgin, published on its website a top-ten list of his favorite leadership quotes on November 24, 2014, where number 1 is the quote examined here. He wrote "the ability" instead of "your ability," otherwise it's the same wording, and he accredited it to Lao Tzu.

Maybe he read Robert A. Leo's book mentioned above, and got the accreditation wrong. He also had this quote in his book *The Virgin Way*, published in September the same year.

December 19 he posted the same quote on his Twitter account, where he accidentally spelled the Chinese philosopher's name "Lao Tuz." It is possible that he misspelled the name also on his top-ten list, but corrected it later. His tweet was retweeted 1,200 times. A number of repetitions of the quote on other websites had the faulty spelling of Lao Tzu's name, making it clear where they got it from.

Another Lao Tzu quote by Richard Branson is discussed in the chapter "The heart that gives."

Life and death are one thread

"Life and death are one thread, the same line viewed from different sides."

It amazes me that this quote ever got attributed to Lao Tzu. He was definitely not the one to speculate about death and its possible meaning or nature. He made no claim in *Tao Te Ching* of death being anything but the abrupt end of life.

The quote makes little or no sense. If it said birth and death it would be understandable. At birth you have that long line of life in front of you, whereas at the point of death you have it behind you. Not that it is anything more than a truism, but it is still undeniable.

Lao Tzu played with truisms in *Tao Te Ching*, but he took them somewhere. He made them reveal profound things. But this quote is just a statement of the obvious – at best. Its wording really makes it completely meaningless.

But you will find out that there is a twist to this story.

I could not find a *Tao Te Ching* version containing this quote. I can't even imagine what lines in the text might be misinterpreted in this way. I suspect it is just a quote from wherever, attributed to Lao Tzu by someone along the way.

Checking Facebook, I found no occurrence of the quote until a post from March 28, 2011. It stated Lao Tzu as the author. There was a meme posted as well. I don't know if it was made by the one posting it (Maria Manalang) or not.

There were a couple of more quotes on Facebook each year from 2013 and 2016 (none in 2012), and in 2017 there was suddenly a bundle of them – although my search was done already at the end of March that year.

Several years earlier, though, the quote appeared in printed literature. *Treasury of Spiritual Wisdom: A Collection of 10,000 Inspirational Quotations* from 1996, by Andy Zubko, has the exact quote and accredits it to Lao Tzu (page 88), giving no source to it.

There are six other Lao Tzu quotes in the book, five of which are equally doubtful – among them the "Kindness in words" quote (page 283) and the "There are many paths" quote (page 128), discussed in the chapters with those names. The others are:

No one will attack a person unless he appears to be an enemy. (page 123)

All behavior consists of opposites... Learn to see things backward, inside out, and upside down. (page 113)

To be in mental quiet is to observe the mind's own nature. (page 429)

It is only because the sage does nothing that he can do everything. (page 334)

The last one of them is the only quote that is true to Lao Tzu's thinking, actually at the base of it – referring to the principle of *wu-wei*, non-action.

But there is an earlier source to the quote examined here, and it excuses Andy Zubko's mistake. It can be found in *Chuang Tsu: Inner Chapters* from 1974, translated by Gia-fu Feng and Jane English. They also made a widespread translation of *Tao Te Ching*, discussed in the chapters "He who controls others" and "Knowing others."

Chuang Tzu was a prominent Taoist, second only to Lao Tzu, who lived in the 4th century BC. Here is the passage of the Chuang Tzu text, where a man called No-toes discusses Confucius' shortcomings with Lao Tzu (page 101):

Lao Tsu said, "Why don't you simply let him see that life and death are one thread, the same line seen from different sides – and thus free him from his cuffs and fetters? Is that possible?"

In James Legge's translation of *Chuang Tzu* from 1891 the same quote reads (page 229):

Why did you not simply lead him to see the unity of life and death, and that the admissible and inadmissible belong to one category, so freeing him from his fetters? Would this be possible?

Burton Watson's version from 1964 reads (page 68):

Why don't you just make him see that life and death are the same story, that acceptable and unacceptable are on a single string? Wouldn't it be well to free him from his handcuffs and fetters?

The translations vary and show a complexity of the saying that is lacking in the short quote examined here, but they are still somewhat corresponding.

In conclusion, then, the origin of the quote is Chuang Tzu – or his students writing his words down. So, although it is not to be found in *Tao Te Ching*, it is hard to deny as a Lao Tzu quote, after all. And it is far too late to discuss with Chuang Tzu to what extent the quote is a true representation of Lao Tzu's ideas.

The quote belongs to the 5th book of Chuang Tzu, called "The Seal of Virtue Complete" in Legge's translation, which belongs to the seven so-called inner chapters. These are the ones generally assumed to have been written by Chuang Tzu, but this is difficult to ascertain. Also, it can be debated what source Chuang Tzu might have had to what Lao Tzu said outside of the words of *Tao Te Ching*.

Still, the possibility of it being a genuine Lao Tzu quote cannot be dismissed, though the wording about life and death being one thread might not be the most accurate translation.

Life is a series

"Life is a series of natural and spontaneous changes. Don't resist them – that only creates sorrow. Let reality be reality. Let things flow naturally forward in whatever way they like."

The first sentence in this quote is modern in form, but still not that strange to the Chinese mind at the time of Lao Tzu. Already back then *I Ching* (*The Book of Change*) was a classic. Its title suggests that everything changes and nothing can be expected to stay the same forever.

Well, things change but the cosmic order by which that happens does not. *Tao*, the Way, was to Lao Tzu the principle behind it all, ever present and ever the same. He certainly saw this process as natural, but hardly spontaneous. To him, it was as fixed – and therefore predictable – as we regard what we call the natural laws.

Because *Tao* is simply the way things work in the world, it would be pointless to resist. Trying to change this only leads to damage and failure. Chapter 29 of *Tao Te Ching* states (my version):

> *Conquering the world and changing it,*
> *I do not think it can succeed.*
> *The world is a sacred vessel that cannot be changed.*
> *He who changes it will destroy it.*
> *He who seizes it will lose it.*

The third sentence of the quote examined here, though, is so superfluous that it becomes odd. What could reality be but reality? The quote would be better without this sentence. Lao Tzu might even wonder what it could mean, since he never discussed either reality's opposite or absence. To him, it was a given. He might instead use the concept of 'ten thousand things,' which I and many others translate to 'the world,' indicating everything in the world. And of course, the world is what it is.

It is interesting that the last sentence of the quote suggests we should let things flow, since Lao Tzu liked to compare *Tao* to water. Chapter 8 of *Tao Te Ching* reads:

> *Supreme good is like water.*
> *Water greatly benefits all things, without conflict.*
> *It flows through places that people loathe.*
> *Thereby it is close to the Way.*

So, the quote discussed here is close, but no cigar. That still means it might be a free paraphrasing or interpretation of something from *Tao Te Ching*.

The earliest occurrence of this quote I have found in a book is already from 1967: *The Mystic Path to Cosmic Power*, by Vernon Howard (page 112). But the wording is a bit different:

> *Life is a series of natural and spontaneous changes. Don't resist them; don't wish things were different. That only creates sorrow. Go along. Let reality be reality. Let things flow naturally forward in whatever way they like. Be like a pebble carried effortlessly along the stream of life.*

Howard makes it clear that he is not quoting, but explaining with his own words what he regards as Taoism's teaching. He mentions both Lao Tzu and Chuang Tzu, but makes no claim to lend the words of either. And it is clear that he knows the distinction. On page 80 of the same book he puts a saying within quotes and accredits it to Lao Tzu: "Perfect kindness acts without thinking of kindness." That quote, by the way, is discussed in the chapter "Perfect kindness" of this book.

Anyway, it is safe to say that the quote discussed here originates with Vernon Howard, though reproduced in a slightly shortened form.

The first book after Howard's to use the quote, as far as I have found, does so with the exact shortened wording of the quote examined here, and accredits it to Lao Tzu. It is *A Guide for the Advanced Soul* from 1985, by Susan Hayward (page 17). This revised quote, attributed to Lao Tzu, was repeated in several books the following decades, and then on the Internet.

Loss is not as bad

"Loss is not as bad as wanting more."

This is a confusing statement. A loss is followed by wanting it back, or it is no loss to mention. So, does the quote mean that it is bad to want more than what one just lost? Maybe what is intended is the curse of the notorious gambler – desperately betting more to regain what was lost, and then some. That fever has ruined many.

In business the principle is pretty much the reverse. You need to accept losses in order to make profit. Focusing too much on diminishing costs will not increase income.

On the other hand, there is the Buddhist principle of doing away with cravings to end suffering, and the Christian tradition of greed being one of the seven deadly sins. Jesus explained to the rich young man, wanting to know how to assure eternal life (Mark 10:21-22, King James Version):

> *One thing thou lackest: go thy way, sell whatsoever thou hast, and give to the poor, and thou shalt have treasure in heaven: and come, take up the cross, and follow me. And he was sad at that saying, and went away grieved: for he had great possessions.*

Lao Tzu also rejected greed very firmly. He found it particularly deplorable in rulers. Chapter 53 of *Tao Te Ching* states (my version):

When the palace is magnificent,
The fields are filled with weeds,
And the granaries are empty.
Some have lavish garments,
Carry sharp swords,
And feast on food and drink.
They possess more than they can spend.
This is called the vanity of robbers.
It is certainly not the Way.

His warning against greed applied not only to the mighty, but to everyone. Those who want more are never satisfied, so it is better to have modest needs. Chapter 46 says:

There is no greater crime than desire.
There is no greater disaster than discontent.
There is no greater misfortune than greed.
Therefore:
To have enough of enough is always enough.

This part of chapter 46 is actually where the quote examined here is from, in a 2009 book called *Soft Like Water: Wisdom of the Tao Te Ching*, by Dale A. Johnson. The book presentation reads: "This is a modified translation of the Tao Te Ching with special regard to the reasons Christians and others should read this literature of wisdom."

Christians and others – doesn't that mean everyone? Anyway, here is his wording of the above quoted part of chapter 46 (page 60):

Natural disasters are not as bad as not knowing what
is enough.
Loss is not as bad as wanting more.

Therefore the sufficiency that comes from knowing what is enough is an eternal sufficiency.

He seems to have missed the line about desire, and there is a lot to be said about how he interpreted the lines he included. Here is D. C. Lau's version from 1963 (page 107):

There is no crime greater than having too many desires;
There is no disaster greater than not being content;
There is no misfortune greater than being covetous.
Hence in being content, one will always have enough.

The main problem with the quote examined here is that the concept of loss is not discussed in this chapter of *Tao Te Ching*. For that perspective, chapter 44 is more relevant (my version):

Greed is costly.
Assembled fortunes are lost.
Those who are content suffer no disgrace.

One thing that confused me about Johnson's book is that on Goodreads, the quote discussed here got its first like on October 11, 2008, the year before the book was published. Amazon specifies its publication as September 30, 2009, by which time the quote had already gotten eight likes on Goodreads. Either Johnson had posted his book, or parts of it, on the web beforehand, or he got the quote from a previous source.

On a website containing multiple translations of *Tao Te Ching* I found that of Charles Muller, where the wording of the whole chapter 46 is the same as Johnson's, except that the latter changed "Tao" to "the Way" (not in the part quoted here). I have checked here and there in the texts, and it seems Johnson has copied Muller all through, with only the "Tao" replacement done.

The webpage with the Muller version is not dated, but it has not been changed since August 4, 2001, so it precedes Johnson's book with at least eight years.

Charles Muller, professor emeritus at the University of Tokyo, is a merited translator and expert on East Asian philosophy and religion. He has his own website (acmuller.net) with several of his translations online, including that of *Tao Te Ching*, which he translated the first time in 1991.

He seems to continue to edit it. His webpage was updated as late as January 23, 2019, but I don't know to what extent. It has a slightly different wording of chapter 46 from what Johnson seems to have copied. Here is his present version of the part of the chapter quoted above:

There is no greater disaster as bad as not knowing what is enough.
No greater than not wanting more.

Therefore the sufficiency that comes from knowing what is enough is an eternal sufficiency.

I don't understand the second sentence of it, which is the one correlating to the quote examined here. It seems to say that not wanting more is a great disaster, but Lao Tzu would really claim the opposite. Did Muller add that "not" accidentally? I bet it is a typo. Anyway, he has abandoned the "loss" of some previous version, which I am all for.

His translation of *Tao Te Ching* was also published as a book in 2005, which did not come up in my web searches on the quote. But I could find it on Amazon, so now it is in my possession. The copyright page of it states that Muller's translation was "written in 1991 and revised in 1997."

Its version of chapter 46 is identical with the one found on the website with multiple *Tao Te Ching* versions mentioned above (oddly, there is no page numbering of the part of the book containing the translation, though there is before and after it).

Another example of Charles Muller's version is discussed briefly in the chapter "Act without expectation."

Love is a decision

"Love is a decision – not an emotion."

Lao Tzu did not discuss love much, and nothing about the amorous love between two persons suggested by this quote. In my version of *Tao Te Ching*, the word "love" is used only twice, and none of them is about love in the conventional sense. In chapter 13 it refers to caring for the world as much as for oneself:

> *He who loves his body as much as the world*
> *Can be entrusted with the world.*

In chapter 17 it is about the people's feelings towards their ruler:

> *The supreme rulers are hardly known by their subjects.*
> *The lesser are loved and praised.*
> *The even lesser are feared.*
> *The least are despised.*

The idea to regard love as a decision more than an emotion is from the psychoanalyst and sociologist Erich Fromm (1900-1980) in his book *The Art of Loving* from 1956. He wrote about a love that is committed and intended to last (page 56):

To love somebody is not just a strong feeling — it is a decision, it is a judgment, it is a promise. If love were only a feeling, there would be no basis for the promise to love each other forever. A feeling comes and it may go. How can I judge that it will stay forever, when my act does not involve judgment and decision?

In later literature it has been shortened to the quote discussed here. The earliest example of this I have found is in *The Healing Energies of Music* from 1983, by Hal Lingerman. He paraphrased Fromm, naming *The Art of Loving* as his source. Later books with this quote mention neither Fromm nor anyone else as the source.

Also on the Internet the quote started to appear years ago, without any accreditation. Around the year 2013 the reference to Lao Tzu started to appear, mainly in memes. In July that year, the quote got its first like on Goodreads, where it was also accredited to Lao Tzu.

My guess is that the accreditation to Lao Tzu happened rather haphazardly. The quote was around years before, and somewhere along the way it was starting to get linked to Lao Tzu, just to set a fancy name to it.

Love is of all passions the strongest

"Love is of all passions the strongest, for it attacks simultaneously the head, the heart, and the senses."

A quote about love is very unlikely to be from Lao Tzu. He had no treatment of it in its conventional sense, that of two people connecting. In my version of *Tao Te Ching* the word appears only twice – one of them about loving oneself as much as the world (chapter 13) and the other about rulers loved by their subjects (chapter 17). Passion is not mentioned even once. This was simply not a subject Lao Tzu covered.

Furthermore, the perspective of how a passion "attacks" a person, be it the head, heart, or senses, Lao Tzu would probably find revolting. His idea was calm acceptance of the way the world works.

The oldest book I have found with this exact quote is *World's Wit and Wisdom* from 1936, reprinted in 1945, by Norman Lockridge (page 142). He ascribed the quote to the French 18th century philosopher Voltaire, without specifying the source. The book also contains three pages of Lao Tzu quotes, again without stating the source.

Lockridge's reference led me to Voltaire's *Thoughts, Remarks, and Observations*, a translation from the French, published in 1802. That was just 24 years after his death. The collection of Voltaire comments and thoughts was compiled after his death, from unpublished material he left behind. The exact words of the quote are there (page 9).

The first book I have found accrediting the quote to Lao Tzu is *Chinese Sexual Astrology* from 2006, by Shelly Wu (page ii and the back cover). She gave no source to her claim. Other books would follow with the same accreditation. And of course, web pages and memes in great numbers.

From one great thinker to another, two thousand years backwards – that is quite a journey for a quote.

Make your heart like a lake

"Make your heart like a lake with a calm, still surface and great depths of kindness."

In the Chinese tradition, the heart as a symbol is not the same as in the Western world. Where we talk of it as the seat of emotions, the Chinese link it to the mind and the will. Therefore, English versions of *Tao Te Ching* usually translate the word to 'mind' instead of writing 'heart.' Otherwise, the readers would be misled.

For example, this line in chapter 8 contains the pictogram for the heart where I use the word 'mind' in my version, and so do most translations of it:

A good mind is deep.

Nor did Lao Tzu write about a lake, but he did mention water more than once. Water was to him an ideal, because of how it yields by floating to the lowest grounds. Thereby, it is comparable to *Tao*, the Way. Chapter 8, quoted above, also states:

Supreme good is like water.
Water greatly benefits all things, without conflict.
It flows through places that people loathe.
Thereby it is close to the Way.

So, the depth of the mind should be compared to the low places to which water goes, where the nature of *Tao* is to be found, too. And in chapter 12 Lao Tzu warned against over-stimulating the mind:

Racing through the field and hunting make the mind wild.

Indeed the mind should be both calm and deep, as the quote examined here claims about the heart. Kindness, too, was something Lao Tzu propagated, though not with the same words. In chapter 5 he even seemed to discard kindness:

Heaven and Earth are not kind.
They regard all things as offerings.
The sage is not kind.
He regards people as offerings.

Still, he said in chapter 8:

A good gift is kind.

Furthermore, the chapter states that words should be sincere and rulers just. Chapter 10 explains how people should be treated:

To give birth to them and nourish them,
Carry them without taking possession of them,
Care for them without subduing them,
Raise them without steering them.
That is the greatest virtue.

The sage has to be caring, chapter 27 insists:

The sage takes care of all people,
Forsaking no one.
He takes care of all things,
Forsaking nothing.
This is called following the light.

Caring is not the same as kindness, which clarifies the harsh words in chapter 5. Being kind means little more than letting people do as they please, whether it is good for them or not, while caring for them means helping them find a better path and protecting them while they proceed on it.

In spite of the above, the quote examined here is indeed from a version of *Tao Te Ching*. The exact wording is from *Lao Tzu's Tao Te Ching* by Timothy Freke, from 1995. It is in his interpretation of chapter 8. Freke has followed the standard translations in the first section and the last line of the chapter, but in between he goes his very own way:

Make your heart like a lake,
with a calm, still surface,
and great depths of kindness.

Nurture your true nature.
Make love your gift to others.
Only talk the truth.

Flow around obstacles, don't confront them.
Don't struggle to succeed.
Wait for the right moment.

For comparison, here is my version of the same section:

A good dwelling is on the ground.
A good mind is deep.
A good gift is kind.
A good word is sincere.
A good ruler is just.
A good worker is able.
A good deed is timely.

And here is that of D. C. Lau from 1963 (page 64):

In a home it is the site that matters;
In quality of mind it is depth that matters;
In an ally it is benevolence that matters;
In speech it is good faith that matters;
In government it is order that matters;
In affairs it is ability that matters;
In action it is timeliness that matters.

Freke mostly followed the general form of listing Lao Tzu's preferences, but the content differs considerably. Where Lao Tzu was concrete and practical, Freke went personal and vague. The lines are like advice from a self-realization manual with poetic ambitions.

I wonder, what are depths of kindness and what is your true nature? As for love, it was not something Lao Tzu cared to explore in his text. Freke would have done better to stay as close to the original as he did in the other parts of the chapter.

In the introduction to his book, he explained how he reached his wordings:

My method has been to meditate upon many different, often divergent, translations of a chapter, until it began to speak to me in a direct and simple way.

Well, the standard translations are both simpler and more direct. He just managed to make yet another divergent version.

By the way, there is another quote circulating on the web, rather similar to the one discussed here:

If you make your heart like a lake, life will continuously fulfill you.

It is linked to the *I Ching* book of divination and its 55th hexagram in The *Essential I Ching: 64 Degrees of Nature's Wisdom* from 2015, by Kari Hohne (page 385), and also in her book *Nothing Bad Happens in Life: Nature's Way of Success* from 2009 (page 151).

I have not found this or any similar wording about that hexagram in the other versions of *I Ching* I checked, but that goes beyond the scope of this book.

Kari Hohne has also written a version of the Lao Tzu classic: *Tao Te Ching: The Poetry of Nature* from 2009. But her wording of chapter 8 stays quite close to the standard translations (page 19).

Man's enemies are not demons

"Man's enemies are not demons, but human beings like himself."

Lao Tzu would laugh at this statement. Of course men are not demons. They can't be, since they are human beings. Not that Lao Tzu cared much at all for supernatural beings, not even deities, but he could tell the difference. He would regard the quote as pure nonsense.

Stephen Mitchell, author of a very popular version of *Tao Te Ching* from 1988, obviously sees it differently. The quote is from his rendering of chapter 31, with the slight difference of writing "his" instead of "man's." That's surely an edit when the quote was taken out of its context.

But Mitchell's version is so far off from the original that I have trouble seeing what line he interpreted this way. Here is the relevant part of Mitchell's chapter 31, listing what "a decent man" prefers:

> *Peace is his highest value.*
> *If the peace has been shattered,*
> *how can he be content?*
> *His enemies are not demons,*
> *but human beings like himself.*
> *He doesn't wish them personal harm.*
> *Nor does he rejoice in victory.*
> *How could he rejoice in victory*
> *and delight in the slaughter of men?*

Here is my version of the same part, referring to the preferences of "the noble ruler":

Peace and quiet are preferred.
Victory should not be praised.
Those who praise victory relish manslaughter.
Those who relish manslaughter
Cannot reach their goals in the world.

And here is James Legge's version from 1891 (page 74), speaking about "the superior man":

Calm and repose are what he prizes; victory (by force of arms) is to him undesirable. To consider this desirable would be to delight in the slaughter of men; and he who delights in the slaughter of men cannot get his will in the kingdom.

Mitchell has allowed himself to expand with his own words on why the enemy should not be despised, which may be commendable but also unnecessary in this context. Lao Tzu did not feel the need to explain that enemies are people, too. What else could they be? Instead he focused on the importance of regarding war with grief and regret, even when it is won.

For more about Stephen Mitchell and his version of *Tao Te Ching*, see the chapter "A good traveler has no fixed plans."

Marriage is three parts love

"Marriage is three parts love and seven parts forgiveness of sins."

Lao Tzu did not write about marriage and marital love at all. Nor would he be comfortable with the word "sin," which is something closely linked to Christianity. Still, this quote is frequently accredited to him – I fail to see why.

It is, in fact, from a play called *The New York Idea* by Langdon Elwyn Mitchell (1862-1935). It premiered 1906, and was published in a book 1908. John, one of the characters of the play, speaks bitterly about his former wife (pages 62-63):

Well, she was an heiress, an American heiress — and she'd been taught to think marriage meant burnt almonds and moonshine and a yacht and three automobiles, and she thought — I don't know what she thought, but I tell you, Mrs. Phillimore, marriage is three parts love and seven parts forgiveness of sins.

This comment about love and sins has been quoted in many books through the years, ascribing it to its proper author. The first book to ascribe it to Lao Tzu, as far as I have found, is *Making a Short Speech or Toast* from 2016, by Jackie Arnold. I have not been able to check its first edition from 2007, but I assume the quote was there as well.

The earliest web page I have found accrediting the

quote to Lao Tzu is in a comment from February 25, 2011, on a blog post on temptation and sin. It appeared on Facebook for the first time the same year, ascribing it correctly to Mitchell. The following year, on April 26, 2012, the first Facebook post ascribing it to Lao Tzu appeared.

I am not convinced that ascribing the quote to Lao Tzu originated with Arnold's book, but I have not found any earlier source to it. Why anyone would imagine this to be a genuine Lao Tzu quote remains a mystery.

Most of the world's religions

"Most of the world's religions serve only to strengthen attachments to false concepts such as self and other, life and death, heaven and earth, and so on. Those who become entangled in these false ideas are prevented from perceiving the Integral Oneness."

What would Lao Tzu, who lived in China around 2,400 years ago, know about the world's religions? He was not even that interested in deities and such of his time and place. He mentioned one specific deity in *Tao Te Ching*, only in passing, while contemplating the origin of *Tao* (chapter 4, my version):

> *I do not know whose child it is.*
> *It seems to precede the ancestor of all.*

This ancestor of all was *Ti*, supreme god in Chinese mythology, who was regarded as the creator. Still, Lao Tzu indicated that *Tao* was older, which means existing before the creation of the world. In other words, even the creator god had to obey the laws of *Tao*.

The only other mention of deities in *Tao Te Ching* is in chapter 39, where it lists what entities obtained unity with the One, which is *Tao*. Among them were the spirits, who became deities by it, and thereby avoided withering.

The concept of religion is in itself of much later origin, getting its present meaning from the Renaissance and on, when other beliefs than the Christian one were increasingly explored. In ancient China, the term would have had little meaning, especially in plural.

Moving on through the quote, Lao Tzu would definitely not agree that the concepts of heaven and earth were false. He mentioned them frequently in *Tao Te Ching*, as opposites making up the world. In chapter 5 he wrote:

> *Is not the space between Heaven and Earth like a bellows?*
> *It is empty, but lacks nothing.*
> *The more it moves, the more comes out of it.*

The "Integral Oneness" ending the quote examined here is a strange expression. It must refer to *Tao*, the Way, but does so in a more complicated manner than necessary or relevant. What does it even mean? I would assume that an integral one consists of more than one, and therefore is not only one. Lao Tzu sometimes called *Tao* "the One," for example in chapter 10:

> *Can you make your soul embrace the One*
> *And not lose it?*

The quote examined here is not from *Tao Te Ching*, but from *Hua Hu Ching: The Unknown Teachings of Lao Tzu* from 1992 (paperback edition 1995), interpreted by Brian Browne Walker (chapter 16, page 19).

Hua Hu Ching is a text falsely claimed to be by Lao Tzu, though composed hundreds of years later, which only exists in fragments discovered as late as 1900. For more about it, read the chapter "Embrace all things."

An earlier version than Walker's of *Hua Hu Ching* was written by Hua-Ching Ni, first published in 1979: *The Com-*

plete Works of Lao Tzu: Tao Teh Ching and Hua Hu Ching. It is not based on the old fragments of the text, but on "education from my parents" (page 105). Walker readily confessed his dependence on it, but Ni's wording of the same quote is different (page 121):

> *Many people are pleased and satisfied with the various limited religious doctrines existing in the world today. They all hope to live in the kingdom of Heaven someday and sit sublimely at the side of their personal deity, but by entertaining such hopes and beliefs they only foster concepts of self and others, longevity and brevity, life and death, and so on without end. With such conceptual entanglements they cannot even listen to the truth, much less study, practice and embrace it or explain it to others. In this case, how can they ever uplift themselves to the subtle, central realm to be with the Universal One of One Universal Life?*

So, none of the quotes is based on an ancient text and can in no way be said to contain the words of Lao Tzu. Still, the quote has frequently been passed on as a saying of his, as things go. Lately, memes have played a significant part in this.

Music in the soul

"Music in the soul can be heard by the universe."

This cryptic statement has a poetic flare that inspires contemplation — but as a Lao Tzu quote, three of its words raise questions: music, soul, and universe. Neither of them fits his vocabulary that well.

As for music, Lao Tzu seems not to have given it much thought. The word appears only once in *Tao Te Ching*, and that's in passing. It's in chapter 35 (my version):

Music and food make the traveler halt.
But words spoken about the Way have no taste.

So, Lao Tzu states that music has no significance in the grand scale of things.

The soul, as we know it, is mainly a concept of Christian belief. Lao Tzu did not separate the mind into different entities, and regarded it as completely locked to the body. There is no claim of an afterlife in *Tao Te Ching*.

In my version of the text, the word is mentioned only once, and I think I should really have used some other term – if I could find one more accurate. It is at the start of chapter 10, where Lao Tzu lists abilities that a true sage should have:

Can you make your soul embrace the One
And not lose it?

Other translations also use "soul" and D. C. Lau had this explanation of it in a footnote (page 66):

Man has two souls, the p'o which is the soul of the body and the hun which is the soul of the spirit. After death, the p'o descends into earth while the hun ascends into heaven.

That may sound like some kind of afterlife, or actually two, but Lao Tzu did not make any other mention of it, nor did he seem the least bit interested in supernatural beliefs of ancient China regarding human immortality. Well, with one additional exception, in chapter 60 (my version):

When the world is ruled according to the Way,
The ghosts lose their power.
The ghosts do not really lose their power,
But it is not used to harm people.

The ghosts were *kuei*, restless spirits of deceased ancestors.

Thirdly, the word universe implies an understanding of a vast space in which our planet is in no way the middle, nor the place where it all began. In the time of Lao Tzu, that would be a stretch of the imagination, indeed. He spoke about the world, meaning the earth we walk on and the heaven we see when we look up. And this world he spoke about a lot, certainly.

But even with a wording more accurate to Lao Tzu's understanding, some kind of internal music heard by the world would make little sense to him – or us. Is it a hint at telepathy of some sort? Or should it be interpreted as symbol for inner joy, concluding that happiness is contagious? I think Lao Tzu would frown at the idea. Although obviously humorous, he was no entertainer. In his world, events were caused by people's actions, not their moods.

The origin of this quote is a difficult one to trace. The first mention of it I found on Facebook is from July 21, 2009, accrediting it to Lao Tzu. Next year it appeared five times, two of which accredited it to Lao Tzu. Since then the quote, with the Lao Tzu reference, has spread modestly on Facebook, increasingly by meme images.

Slightly earlier, on January 10, 2009, the quote got its first like on the Goodreads website, also accrediting it to Lao Tzu. By now (August 2020) it has received 666 likes, which is a number with its own symbolic significance. A Google search (August 2020) gives almost 70,000 hits with the exact wording of the quote.

There are several printed books containing the exact quote, the oldest of which is *Kung Fu Meditations & Chinese Proverbial Wisdom*, by Ellen Kei Hua, first published in 1973 and revised 1974. A major part of the book consists of 41 quotes called "meditations," where the 37th is the quote discussed here.

Unfortunately there is no source specified for any of the quotes, but the introduction states that *Tao Te Ching*, Chuang Tzu, *I Ching*, and "other Chinese and Eastern sages" have been used. Many of the quotes are indeed from *Tao Te Ching* – but not this one.

Nor is this quote from Chuang Tzu, but there is something similar in his Book 14, "The Revolution of Heaven," translated by James Legge in 1891 (page 349):

> *The Perfect Music first had its response in the affairs of men, and was conformed to the principles of Heaven; it indicated the action of the five virtues, and corresponded to the spontaneity (apparent in nature).*

And two pages later in the same Book (page 351) there is something called "the music of Heaven, delighting the mind without the use of words."

That is still quite far from the quote examined here.

My teachings

"My teachings are easy to understand
and easy to put into practice.
Yet your intellect will never grasp them,
and if you try to practice them, you'll fail.

My teachings are older than the world.
How can you grasp their meaning?

If you want to know me,
look inside your heart."

These pompous and arrogant words are far from the mentality of Lao Tzu. What the quote says is that we should all give it up, because we have no chance to grasp the message. Instead we should settle for looking inside our hearts. Under these circumstances, what can we expect to find there but despair?

There is a contradiction between the first line about the teachings being easy to understand, and the following lines dismissing our ability to do so. Lao Tzu liked to use paradoxes, but not contradictions. Also, he warned repeatedly against showing off and putting oneself above others.

This quote is easily connected to a certain chapter from *Tao Te Ching*, although it is an unpleasant distortion of its wording and message. It is a rendition of chapter 70, which in my version reads like this:

My words are very easy to understand
And very easy to practice.
Still, no one in the world
Can understand or practice them.

My words have an origin.
My deeds have a sovereign.
Truly, because people do not understand this,
They do not understand me.

That so few understand me is why I am treasured.
Therefore, the sage wears coarse clothes, concealing jade.

Robert G. Henricks in 1989 used clarifications found in the Mawangdui manuscripts from around 200 BC to come up with his version:

My words are easy to understand,
And easy to put into practice.
Yet no one in the world can understand them,
And no one can put them into practice.
Now my words have an ancestor, and my deeds have a lord,
And it's simply because [people] have no understanding [of them],
that they therefore don't understand me.
But when those who understand me are few, then I'm of great value.
Therefore the Sage wears coarse woolen cloth, but inside it he holds on to jade.

The similarities between the quote examined here and the two versions of chapter 70 are obvious, but also the differences. Already by choosing 'teachings' instead of 'words,' the quote's attitude of superiority is enhanced. The same goes for the statement about 'intellect,' a modern concept which is out of place in a text from ancient China. It implies an inability that is not possible to overcome, especially since the word 'never' is added. If someone would still have hope, it is whisked away with the line about failure for those who still try.

What Lao Tzu states is not that people try and fail, but that they don't even try because they don't understand. Why would one even try to practice something one doesn't understand? The lines are not a doom on human capacity, but on our awareness. A modern wording would be something like: we don't know what's best for us.

That is what Lao Tzu explains in the following lines. He understands because he is connected to the origin and sovereign, which is *Tao*, the Way. Those who have no connection with *Tao* are unable to understand Lao Tzu when he speaks about it or acts in accordance with it. If they were to grasp it, and Lao Tzu does not deny the possibility, they would understand him.

The quote examined here, on the other hand, doesn't grant people that option. It states bluntly that we are unable to grasp the meaning. If so, what would be the point of even trying?

In the last two lines, the quote suggests that Lao Tzu would still be possible to know, if we look into our hearts. The symbolic meaning of the heart differs between the East and the West. To the former, it signifies the mind and willpower, whereas to us it is mainly about emotions – especially in an expression of this kind. It claims that we should search our feelings for the answer.

Lao Tzu would not agree. *Tao* is something for the mind to ponder and discover. The end of the chapter deals not with how to understand him, but with the value he possesses by his insight – and that he should still be modest. The quote discussed here omits this, elevating Lao Tzu to something akin to a deity.

The quote is from Stephen Mitchell's 1988 version of *Tao Te Ching* (page 70), which has been a bestseller for many years. It is very popular for its elegant and straightforward text. Unfortunately, it frequently deviates quite a lot from Lao Tzu's words and the standard interpretations, as can be found in my discussions of several other flawed Lao Tzu quotes coming from his book.

For more about Stephen Mitchell and his version of *Tao Te Ching*, see the chapter "A good traveler has no fixed plans."

Nature is not human-hearted

"Nature is not human-hearted."

Human-hearted is a weird expression. Human hearts can be of so many kinds, whether we mean emotions or mentality. It is hard to figure out what would be a quality of the heart shared by the whole species.

But there is a Chinese word sometimes translated with the expression human-hearted: *ren*, which means to be humane, benevolent, or simply kind. It was used as an ideal by Confucius and other ancient Chinese thinkers, including Lao Tzu.

For example, chapter 5 of *Tao Te Ching* starts with the following lines (my version):

Heaven and Earth are not kind.
They regard all things as offerings.
The sage is not kind.
He regards people as offerings.

The word 'kind' is *ren* in the original text. These lines have caused some concern among interpreters, since it seems to imply that Heaven and Earth as well as the sage are all indifferent to human suffering, even ruthless.

In a way, that is true. Lao Tzu pointed out that there is a grand scale of things in which individual needs do not matter. *Tao* works in its own manner, whatever we think about it or might hope for. In the grand order of the world, humans and their fates are really insignificant.

Heaven and Earth are the two parts that together form the whole world. Like the rest of humankind at that time, ancient China had a geocentric view, with the earth in the center and everything visible of the cosmos out there simply being its surroundings. But there were in Lao Tzu's eyes dynamics between Heaven and Earth, described in the same chapter. Between them, all things and lives emerged:

Is not the space between Heaven and Earth like a bellows?
It is empty, but lacks nothing.
The more it moves, the more comes out of it.

It would not be misleading to substitute 'Heaven and Earth' with 'the world,' or for that matter 'nature.' I would not choose the latter, since it would fit better to describe all that comes out of the bellows. But it is doable. So did, for example, C. Spurgeon Medhurst in 1905 (page 9), Lin Yutang in 1948 (page 63), and Wing-tsit Chan in 1963 (page 107).

Then the quote discussed here could be understood as a version of the first line of chapter 5. And it is.

In literature using the quote it has often been referred to as from this chapter. Also in the oldest mentioning of it that I have found in print, which is from 1962. It is in the UNESCO series *Impact of science on society*, XII, 3 (page 194), in an article by Alan Mackay called "An Outsider's View of Science in Japan."

He interpreted the quote to mean that nature was not anthropomorphic in the Taoist perspective, and therefore people of the East have found it easier than those in the West to accept scientific revelations about evolution, heliocentricity, and relativity. That is a bold interpretation, at least in reference to the quote discussed here.

Unfortunately, Mackay did not mention from what

version of *Tao Te Ching* he got the quote, and I have not been able to find it. In his list of references, the one book that seemed plausible to contain the quote – *The Ways of Thinking of Eastern Peoples* from 1960, by Hajime Nakamura – does not.

Maybe Mackay paraphrased some *Tao Te Ching* version, but it is still odd that he would choose the expression "human-hearted." He might have done so to increase the contrast between nature and humans, for the sake of his theory. It is also possible that he made his own translation of the Chinese original, which would have given him the opportunity to find the English expression for *ren* fitting his thoughts the best.

Mackay's article might not have found that many readers, but in 1977 the quote with the same accreditation was published in *The Harvest of a Quiet Eye: a Selection of Scientific Quotations* (page 91). The selection of the quotations had been made by the same Alan Mackay. A new edition was published in 1991 with the shortened title *A Dictionary of Scientific Quotations*.

The quote also found its way into other dictionaries of quotations – and later on, the Internet.

New beginnings

"New beginnings are often disguised as painful endings."

This is a rather complicated way of stating that after rain comes shine. Well, it does have the added meaning that a beginning can seem like an end. Still, it is not something Lao Tzu would have stated.

In his world there was nothing new, and if there was he would be very hesitant to praise it. He talked repeatedly about the need for mankind to return to the ways and wisdom of old. The perspective of endings and new beginnings was simply neither interesting nor relevant to him. The last lines of chapter 14 in *Tao Te Ching* state it clearly (my version):

> Hold on to the ancient Way to master the present,
> And to learn the distant beginning.
> This is called the unbroken strand of the Way.

The quote examined here, falsely accredited to Lao Tzu, appears all over the Internet. I bet it's a quote from someone else, but I have not been able to track its origin.

The first mention of the quote I found on the web was in a blog post from March 15, 2008. It stated Lao Tzu as the author, but gave no reference to the source. The earliest appearance on Facebook was a post from March 29, 2010. It didn't name any author. In 2011, there were suddenly lots of Facebook posts with the quote, and most of them assigning it to Lao Tzu. On Goodreads, where the quote is also ascribed to Lao Tzu, it got its first like in July 2013.

A Google book search shows no mention of the quote before those dates, actually not after them either.

A slight variation of the quote, also accredited to Lao Tzu, is "observe how endings become beginnings." That is from chapter 16 of a version of *Tao Te Ching* in *Living the Wisdom of the Tao*, by Wayne W. Dyer, 2008, page 32. This is how Dyer translated the whole sentence:

Amidst the rush of worldly comings and goings,
observe how endings become beginnings.

It is far from the wording in Lao Tzu's text, but not unfathomable. Here is my version of the same lines:

All things arise in unison.
Thereby we see their return.

Robert G. Henricks in 1989 wrote, using the Chinese expression "ten thousand things," which simply means everything there is (page 218):

The ten thousand things — side-by-side they arise;
And by this I see their return.

Lao Tzu did seem to speak of the cyclic nature of the world. The next lines make it even clearer: "All things flourish, and each returns to its source." But he did not regard this process as painful.

I seriously doubt it, but if there is some strange version of *Tao Te Ching* from which the quote discussed here is fetched, then it is most likely to be of the same lines in chapter 16. But that would still be a wording so far off from Lao Tzu, the quote must be regarded as fake.

For more about Wayne W. Dyer and his interpretations of *Tao Te Ching*, see the chapter "Every human being's essential nature."

One cannot reflect

"One cannot reflect in streaming water. Only those who know internal peace can give it to others."

The idea of only a peaceful person being able to make others peaceful fits well with Lao Tzu's thoughts. He didn't express it exactly like the quote above, but close enough – for example, in chapter 57 of *Tao Te Ching* (my version):

I am at peace,
And people become fair by themselves.

And in chapter 35 the path to peace is described:

Hold on to the great image,
And the whole world follows,
Follows unharmed,
Content and completely at peace.

The great image is *Tao*, the Way. The one who stays with its principle makes others follow and become peaceful. It is possible that this image has been interpreted as a reflection, a mirror, which is indeed an image of sorts. Then the quote discussed here might be described as a free interpretation of the lines from chapter 35.

The earliest example of this exact quote I have found is in the book *One Home, One Family, One Future* from 2009, by B. A. Zikria (page 73). He listed a number of Lao Tzu quotes and stated as his source the website Quotationspage. I have not found that quote there, though, nor some others in Zikria's list. But that is no mystery – web pages change constantly, and this reference is more than a decade old.

So, I used Internet Archive to check versions of that web page from before Zikria's book was published, but with no luck. The content seems to have been the same all through the years. The source to just about all the quotes is Wing-tsit Chan's version of *Tao Te Ching* from 1963, but his book does not contain the quote examined here.

The oldest example of the quote I found on Facebook is a meme posted January 14, 2011, where the quote is accredited to Confucius, not Lao Tzu. That did not stop later posts on Facebook from accrediting it to Lao Tzu.

To be sure, I made a search through James Legge's translations of Confucian texts, without finding the quote. But in *Chuang Tsu: Inner Chapters* from 1974, by Gia-fu Feng and Jane English, Confucius says (page 95):

Men cannot see their reflection in running water but only in still water. Only that which is still in itself can still the seekers of stillness.

It is in Book 5 of Chuang Tzu, "Signs of full virtue," where Confucius discussed a crippled man who attracted many followers although he was still, saying nothing. Legge's wording of this section from Chuang Tzu is different, but the meaning is the same (*The Texts of Taoism*, volume 1, page 225).

Feng and English also wrote a popular version of *Tao Te Ching*, so it is quite plausible that this quote from Chuang Tzu has been spread and paraphrased into the quote examined here, along the way mistakenly accredited to Lao Tzu.

One who is too insistent

"One who is too insistent on his own views finds few to agree with him."

This saying might be true, but it is not from Lao Tzu. He definitely scolded those who regarded themselves as knowledgeable and wanted others to hear it, for example in the 81st and last chapter of *Tao Te Ching* (my version):

Those who are right do not argue.
Those who argue are not right.
Those who know are not learned.
Those who are learned do not know.

He warned that people prone to arguing and flaunting their learning were not to be trusted, even if they might sound convincing. But he also implied that those who really knew would not be listened to, because they did not sound equally convincing. That was indeed his problem. He found few to agree with his words about *Tao*, the Way (chapter 41):

The average student listens to the Way
And follows some and some not.
The lesser student listens to the Way
And laughs out loud.

And in chapter 70 he complained:

My words are very easy to understand
And very easy to practice.
Still, no one in the world
Can understand or practice them.

But to him, it was not a question of promoting his own views. He spoke about *Tao*, the Way, and grieved the fact that so few understood it as he did. Nevertheless, he was not at all to give up his insights, whether others agreed or not. To him it was not about opinion, but realization. Of course it can therefore be said that he insisted on his views, but he was not the one to insist on others to agree with him. He had no urge to agitate.

He did not write *Tao Te Ching* to convert those who rejected his views, but for the ones who would be curious about his perspective. Chapter 41, which is also quoted above, starts:

The superior student listens to the Way
And follows it closely.

Still, the quote examined here is from a version of Lao Tzu's text: *Tao Teh King: Interpreted as Nature and Intelligence* from 1958, by the philosophy professor Archie J. Bahm (1907-1996). As the title points out, he translated *Tao* as Nature, which is unusual but doable. Calling *te* intelligence, on the other hand, is much less credible. The quote is a line from chapter 24 (page 29).

Here is my version of that line:

Those who are self-righteous are not prominent.

James Legge's wording from 1891 comes a bit closer to that of Bahm (page 67):

He who asserts his own views is not distinguished.

And Philip J. Ivanhoe in 2002 wrote (page 24):

Those who affirm their own views are not well-known.

Bahm's version is quite far from these, but not impossibly so. Insisting on one's own views could be understood as considering oneself right, and few agreeing might be compared to lack of prominence.

But it kind of misses the point Lao Tzu wanted to make: it is the attitude that is unbecoming, not the opinion or arguments. People might actually agree, but they would still be offended by the attitude. Bahm would have been closer to Lao Tzu's words if he wrote "few wanting to agree with him."

For more on Archie J. Bahm's version of *Tao Te Ching*, see the chapters "He who controls others" and "Respond intelligently."

Perfect kindness

"Perfect kindness acts without thinking of kindness."

Lao Tzu did not praise kindness, probably because it would be meaningless to him without a higher purpose. True kindness is not just to treat people well, but to help them along. That can sometimes seem unkind. Chapter 5 of *Tao Te Ching* states (my version):

> *Heaven and Earth are not kind.*
> *They regard all things as offerings.*
> *The sage is not kind.*
> *He regards people as offerings.*

What he implied was that everything and everyone are parts of the whole, so individual preferences hardly count. There is a greater order, which is *Tao*, the Way, and even when it doesn't look like it, it is for the best for all. The sage may not be kind, but works for what is good. Chapter 49 explains:

> *The sage has no concern for himself,*
> *But makes the concerns of others his own.*
> *He is good to those who are good.*
> *He is also good to those who are not good.*
> *That is the virtue of good.*

The quote examined here suggests that the best kindness is of the unselfish kind, demanding no praise. Lao Tzu might have approved of that, but only if the kind deeds were in accordance with *Tao*. Otherwise, no matter how kind, they might not be good.

What he stressed was *te*, virtue, the willingness and ability to follow *Tao*. To him, that would be perfect kindness. Chapter 10 says about how people should be treated:

To give birth to them and nourish them,
Carry them without taking possession of them,
Care for them without subduing them,
Raise them without steering them.
That is the greatest virtue.

The earliest occurrence of the exact quote examined here, as far as I have found, is in the book *Men Who Have Walked with God* from 1945, by Sheldon Cheney (page 19). There it is clearly stated that the quote is from Chuang Tzu, but it is in a chapter devoted to "The Poet Lao-Tse," so people getting the quote from this book may easily have mixed it up.

The first book doing so was *Great Thoughts* from 1954, by Queene Ferry Coonley and Charlotte Krum (page 11). That book seems not to have spread widely, though, but so did *The Mystic Path to Cosmic Power* from 1967, with several later editions, by Vernon Howard (page 80). Either he got the quote from the 1954 book, or he also misread Cheney's book.

On the other hand, they both might have had the same source to the quote as Cheney did. Oddly, I have not been able to find the origin of this Chuang Tzu saying, although Cheney indicates clearly that it is an exact quote. I have checked the sources he lists for Chuang Tzu (page 386).

The problem is that in spite of signaling quotes by italics, Cheney admits to making his own versions of both the many Lao Tzu quotes and those of Chuang Tzu (page 387):

To James Legge I am especially indebted, since I used his nearly literal translation, by courteous permission of the Oxford University Press, as basis for my own "versions" of the poems of Lao-Tse herein presented — though I worked with frequent reference to ten other translations. The excerpts from Chuang-Tse also are "after" Legge.

Unfortunately, Cheney did not refer to any specific *Tao Te Ching* or Chuang Tzu chapters when "quoting" them, so they are difficult to trace. The closest I have come to the quote in James Legge's translation is this, in *The Texts of Taoism*, volume 2, 1891 (page 261):

Heaven has no (special feeling of) kindness, but so it is that the greatest kindness comes from It.

That is not from Chuang Tzu, though, but from a much later text: *Yin Fu Ching, Classic of the Harmony of the Seen and the Unseen*, which Legge placed at the 8th century CE.

Well, in any case it is not a Lao Tzu quote. So, let's leave it at that.

Quarrel with a friend

"Quarrel with a friend and you are both wrong."

This saying is sympathetic, but raises the question: would it be fine to quarrel with anyone who is not your friend? Lao Tzu, for one, would surely not think so. There is no point in quarreling, just a lot of noise with little or no positive result.

On the other hand, neither he nor any other philosopher would claim that when two disagree they are both wrong. That is what this quote implies, and any thinker shuns such a statement. Socrates in his dialectic method discussed a subject until everybody agreed that he was right. He was brazen that way. I bet that every philosopher was convinced of being right – ergo, all opposing views must be wrong.

In all his modesty, Lao Tzu was surely the same. He understood *Tao*, the Way, but very few others did. It is abundantly clear in the unusually personal and emotional chapter 20 of *Tao Te Ching*, where the last lines read (my version):

> *Other people are occupied,*
> *I alone am unwilling, like the outcast.*
> *I alone am different from the others,*
> *Because I am nourished by the great mother.*

The great mother is *Tao*, the Way. He felt all alone in perceiving and understanding it.

Although convinced of his own wisdom, he was still

no friend of arguments. They were pointless to him, since nobody else could really comprehend what he had realized. In the very last of the 81 *Tao Te Ching* chapters he wrote:

> *Those who are right do not argue.*
> *Those who argue are not right.*

A modern English expression describes his sentiment adequately: Why bother?

The earliest appearance I have found of the quote examined here is in the book *Words for All Occasions* from 1997, by Glenn Van Ekeren, accrediting it to Lao Tzu without giving a source (page 169). I have not found it in any *Tao Te Ching* version.

There is nothing unique about the message of the quote. Friends should not need to quarrel, but when they do it can get intense, maybe even damage their friendship. The aikido master Koichi Tohei (1920-2011) had a simple explanation to the problem in his book *Aikido in Daily Life* from 1966 (page 158):

> *Often after a quarrel between friends, both say to themselves, "He was wrong, so he has to apologize first. I won't."*

That is one reason for the conclusion of the quote examined here. Both are wrong in the eyes of the other. I doubt, though, that Tohei is a paraphrased origin of this quote. The dilemma of friends quarreling has been known for long. In the novel *Violet* from 1836, by Marianne Dora Malet, one of the characters says (page 210):

> *When friends quarrel, you are quite sure the quarrel is an irreconcilable one.*

Mike Carey, the writer of comic books and novels, wrote in one of the latter, *The Naming of the Beasts* from 2009 (page 99): "Nobody wins when friends quarrel." Henry Fielding (1707-1754) expressed it with additional severity in *The History Of Tom Jones* from 1749 (page 451 in the 1966 edition):

> *The only way when friends quarrel, is to see it out fairly in a friendly manner, as a man may call it, either with fist, or sword, or pistol, according as they like, and then let it be all over.*

There seems to be little hope that the friends by themselves can end the quarrel peacefully, but Seumas MacManus had a solution in *Yourself and the Neighbours* from 1914 (page 90):

> *If friends quarrel, or there be a family fall-out, it is of course your duty to go to them, hear both sides, gently reprove all parties, and make them shake hands in your presence and promise to be henceforth nearer and dearer than ever to one another.*

That is easier said than done.
So, the dilemma is far from new, but Lao Tzu did not comment on it.

Respond intelligently

"Respond intelligently even to unintelligent treatment."

Intelligence is a modern concept, indicating the rather rude idea that people have differently limited mental capacities. Not to mention the very questionable IQ tests, claiming to order people in a scale of intelligence from the lowest to the highest.

This categorization of individual capacity is something that grew out of a swamp – racial biology and the like in the early 20th century. We should have grown away from it after 1945. The whole idea is repulsive.

Historically, the word used was wisdom, implying that it is something to work on, whatever your starting point might be. Everyone can get wiser. That was also the Lao Tzu perspective. Some are foolish to begin with, but everyone can learn.

The fake Lao Tzu quote is also awkward with the expression "unintelligent treatment." What is that, really? We have all experienced uninformed or ignorant response. But unintelligent – who will be the judge?

What is clever to one is but a joke to another. Even Lao Tzu said that, in chapter 41 (my version):

The lesser student listens to the Way and laughs out loud.
If there were no laughter it would not be the Way.

Notice that Lao Tzu did not claim the lesser student is unable to understand – just unwilling.

The wording of the quote examined here suggests that it is of modern making. That could mean a modern interpretation of *Tao Te Ching*, or some other source altogether. Sadly, it is the former.

The quote is from Archie J. Bahm's version of chapter 63 of *Tao Te Ching* (page 57). Bahm was an American professor of philosophy. His *Tao Te Ching* book, with the subtitle "Interpreted as Nature and Intelligence," was published in 1958. It takes a philosopher to love that word...

He deviated quite a lot from Lao Tzu's words to get to it. Here is my version of the same line:

Return animosity with virtue.

James Legge wrote in his version from 1891:

Recompense injury with kindness.

In other words, be noble even when treated rudely. Nothing at all about intelligence. Lao Tzu didn't have that kind of prejudice.

Other Archie J. Bahm quotes are discussed in the chapters "He who controls others" and "One who is too insistent."

One of the memes spreading this fake Lao Tzu quote is additionally amusing, considering it deals with intelligence: It states that Lao Tzu lived 450 BC – 531 BC. But of course, BC years count backwards. That means he would have been born 131 years after he died. Quite an accomplishment even for Lao Tzu.

There is no trustworthy source to the exact years of Lao Tzu's life. Some say he lived in the 6th century BC, some say one or two hundred years later, and some say he probably didn't exist at all.

Silence is a source

"Silence is a source of great strength."

Lao Tzu would surely recommend silence, though not as a source to strength, but to avoid meaningless chatter. The last lines of chapter 5 in *Tao Te Ching* read (my version):

> *A multitude of words is tiresome,*
> *Unlike remaining centered.*

D. C. Lau in 1963 even used the word silence (page 61):

> *Much speech leads inevitably to silence.*
> *Better to hold fast to the void.*

Robert G. Henricks in 1989 pointed out that both Mawangdui manuscripts from around 200 BC used a term for 'learning' instead of 'words' or 'speech' (page 196):

> *Much learning means frequent exhaustion.*
> *That's not so good as holding on to the mean.*

The Chinese character used for the last word is the same as in the name of China, suggesting right in the middle, mean, or center. There is strength in staying right there, but that was not what Lao Tzu pointed out. Rather, one should not get influenced by endless debate and intellectual discussions, which can confuse the mind. In other words, one should trust one's own judgment.

The oldest books I have found with the exact quote examined here are from 2006: *Asya's Laws* by Asya Raines (page 5), just calling it something she had heard, and *The Art of Mingling* by Jeanne Martinet (page 182), accrediting it to Lao Tzu.

Since both occurrences are so recent, it is likely that they got the quote from the Internet. But the oldest example of the quote I have fund with an ascertained date is from the same year as the books – to be precise, April 29, 2006, ascribing it to Lao Tzu. It is a blog in Portuguese about anesthesia, so I doubt it got that much attention.

Changing the order of the wording slightly, though, gives a different result:

Silence is a great source of strength.

That is a quote from *The Tao of Leadership: Lao Tzu's Tao Te Ching Adapted for a New Age* from 1985, by John Heider (1936-2010). As the title suggests, it is a tendentious version of Lao Tzu's classic, where Heider allowed himself considerable deviations from the original.

The quote is from his version of the last lines of chapter 5, mentioned above. The whole comparable part of the chapter is in his writing (page 9):

The leader does not gossip about others or waste breath arguing the merits of competing theories.
Silence is a great source of strength.

Quite different from the other versions of those lines quoted above. Heider's wording relates minutely to Lao Tzu's words.

Well, at least Heider was frank about making his own adaption. He wrote in the introduction (page xii), "it is my own version of the meaning of Lao Tzu's own words." So, it is not really Lao Tzu's own words. Really not.

Heider wrote another book on the *Tao* theme: *The Tao of Daily Living* from 2000. Another quote from Heider's version of *Tao Te Ching* is discussed in the chapter "When I let go of what I am."

Stop leaving

"Stop leaving and you will arrive. Stop searching and you will see. Stop running away and you will be found."

These sentences are not at all far from what Lao Tzu stated in *Tao Te Ching*. Well, they are not spot on, either. As for leaving and arriving, Lao Tzu would rather say that you already are where you should be, so there is nowhere to arrive. His ideal for human life is expressed in chapter 80 (my version):

> *They can see their neighbors.*
> *Roosters and dogs can be heard from there.*
> *Still, they will age and die*
> *Without visiting one another.*

As for being found, he would rather stress the importance of you finding your own bearing in the world ruled by *Tao*, the Way. No one can find that for you.

Still, the quote is not unlikely as a free paraphrasing of something from *Tao Te Ching*.

The earliest occurrence of the exact quote I have found on the web is in a blog post from January 1, 2011, ascribing it to Lao Tzu without giving a source. On the Goodreads website, the quote got its first like a few months later, in June, 2011. The same year is also the first giving the quote in a book, ascribing it to Lao Tzu: *Discover Your Hidden Memory & Find the Real You*, by Menis Yousry (page 190).

But already by the end of 2004, the quote was used in a newspaper astrology column by Rob Breszny, as a guide to Gemini for the following year. On December 30 the column was published in *Eugene Weekly*, and the following day in *The Austin Chronicle*. Breszny also ascribed it to Lao Tzu.

There is one even earlier appearance of the quote in print: the magazine *Monterey Life* from 1987. In it, the quote is presented as what "a Chinese philosopher once wrote," giving additional lines before the quote discussed here. The complete quote reads:

> *Without traveling to foreign lands,*
> *You can learn the way the world is made.*
> *Without stepping on the stars,*
> *You can see how they are arranged.*
> *The farther you go in search of an answer,*
> *The less you will understand.*
> *Stop leaving,*
> *And you will arrive.*
> *Stop searching,*
> *And you will see.*
> *Stop running away,*
> *And you will be found.*

That is obviously a version of chapter 47 in *Tao Te Ching*. Compare it to my version of that chapter:

> *Without stepping out the door,*
> *You can know the world.*
> *Without looking through the window,*
> *You can see Heaven's Way.*
> *The longer you travel, the less you know.*

Therefore:
The sage knows without traveling,
Perceives without looking,
Completes without acting.

Here is Arthur Waley's version of the chapter, from 1934 (page 200):

Without leaving his door
He knows everything under heaven.
Without looking out of his window
He knows all the ways of heaven.
For the further one travels
The less one knows.
Therefore the Sage arrives without going,
Sees all without looking,
Does nothing, yet achieves everything.

The deviations of the *Monterey Life* version from mine and Waley's form a pattern. They take the Taoism out of the quote. Heaven is replaced by the stars, the sage is replaced by a generic "you," and the non-action so central in Lao Tzu's thoughts is replaced by the odd statement of stopping to run away in order to be found.

This indicates a version aimed at making the Lao Tzu text applicable to anyone, without having to contemplate Taoist ideas. But *Monterey Life* is not guilty of that tendentious deviation. Their fault, particularly embarrassing in journalism, was neglecting to mention the source. Their complete quote of the chapter helped me find it.

This is from a version of *Tao Te Ching* by Benjamin Hoff: *The Way to Life: At the Heart of the Tao Te Ching* from 1981. Hoff reached world fame next year by publishing the big bestseller *The Tao of Pooh*, where he made the world of A. A.

Milne's *Winnie the Pooh* explain the thoughts of Lao Tzu. In 1993 he also published *The Te of Piglet*, completing his writing on Taoism.

His handling of Pooh and Piglet can indeed be questioned, and even more so that of Lao Tzu. Hoff allowed himself a lot of freedom when interpreting the *Tao Te Ching*, often even more than the example of chapter 47 indicates. It seems he mainly tried to make both Lao Tzu's text and the books by A. A. Milne his own.

On the other hand, the international success of *The Tao of Pooh* made Lao Tzu and Taoism familiar to a wider audience than ever before. Without it, the exponentially rising popular interest in the words of Lao Tzu since the 1980's would probably not have taken place, at least not with that speed and magnitude.

Another quote from Benjamin Hoff's version of *Tao Te Ching* is discussed in the chapter "When you find the way."

Stop thinking

"Stop thinking, and end your problems."

To stop thinking is not only detrimental to any philosophy – it is impossible, also to Lao Tzu. He repeatedly encouraged the reader to contemplate the order of life and the workings of *Tao*, the Way. His ideal was the sage, who can reason and thereby reveal the true essence of nature.

The ideal of no thinking is more of a Zen thing, with its concept of empty mind – *mushin* in Japanese, which also implies freedom of ambition and longing. It is the basis of Zen meditation: sit and think of nothing.

There are several similarities between Buddhism, especially Zen, and Lao Tzu's Taoism. But not here. Lao Tzu's world was not one to turn away from, but instead to accept as it was. That, too, is easier said than done.

The quote comes from Stephen Mitchell's 1988 version of *Tao Te Ching*, which is notorious for its often very free interpretations of the text. It's the starting line of chapter 20. That, too, is debatable. But first, here is my version of that line:

Abandon knowledge and your worries are over.

James Legge's version from 1891 reads (page 62):

When we renounce learning we have no troubles.

Wing-tsit Chan in 1963 wrote (page 134):

Abandon learning and there will be no sorrow.

Robert G. Henricks in 1989 wrote (page 224):

Eliminate learning and have no undue concern.

It is about acquired knowledge, and not about thinking as such – a most important difference.

Now, regarding placing the line in chapter 20:

Originally, *Tao Te Ching* had no division into 81 chapters. That's a much later edit, probably at the 1st century BC. The number of chapters was to reach the symbolic symmetry of 9 X 9. The consequence has been an additional complication in understanding the text as it was meant. Verses on different subjects have been combined, and some verses have been split up between chapters wrongly, adding confusion for the reader. As if the text was not already difficult to understand.

Of the above quotes, only I and Robert G. Henricks put the line as the last of chapter 19, instead of the start of chapter 20. But it has been an issue of discussion among Lao Tzu translators and commentators for long. I have followed Henricks' strong arguments for this (page 224), which also seem to be confirmed by the two old *Tao Te Ching* manuscripts discovered in Mawangdui, 1973. They are from around 200 BC.

That may have changed with the Guodian findings in the 1990's of *Tao Te Ching* fragments a hundred years older than those of Mawangdui. Examining the Guodian manuscripts in his book from the year 2000, Henricks found clear support in these findings for the line belonging to chapter 20 (page 29).

The final verdict may not be in yet, but in any case the wording of the quote is not affected by what chapter it belongs to. Lao Tzu would have allowed us to continue pondering it. He might even have been amused.

For more about Stephen Mitchell and his version of *Tao Te Ching*, see the chapter "A good traveler has no fixed plans."

Success is as dangerous as failure

"Success is as dangerous as failure. Hope is as hollow as fear."

This quote makes sense and it is similar to statements made in *Tao Te Ching*. That is no wonder, since it is Stephen Mitchell's 1988 version of the first lines of chapter 13. The problem is that Lao Tzu's text discusses other aspects than Mitchell's wording implies, mainly those of fear and vulnerability. Here is my version of the same lines:

> *Praise and disgrace cause fear.*
> *Honor and great distress are like the body.*

Arthur Waley's version from 1934 reads (page 157):

> *Favour and disgrace goad as it were to madness; high rank hurts keenly as our bodies hurt.*

D. C. Lau in 1963 wrote (page 69):

> *Favour and disgrace are things that startle;*
> *High rank is, like one's body, a source of great trouble.*

Mitchell's interpretation of the first sentence is well within the possible, even elegantly so. His second sentence, though, has replaced the link to bodily vulnerability with a perspective on hope and fear that denounces both. That is questionable, indeed, and has no base in Lao Tzu's thoughts – at least not in this chapter.

Chapter 13 goes on explaining what these statements mean, but that is treated in my chapter "Hope and fear are both phantoms," which deals with Mitchell's version of other lines in this same *Tao Te Ching* chapter.

The only reason I at all treat this quote separately is the fact that it appears as such in books and on the web.

For more about Stephen Mitchell and his version of *Tao Te Ching*, see the chapter "A good traveler has no fixed plans."

The best fighter

"The best fighter is never angry."

A fighter? It is bizarre to link a saying about a fighter to Lao Tzu. He was no sports fan, nor a street hoodlum. He did speak about warriors, but far from approvingly, and he condemned violence.

He did admit that war might sometimes be inevitable, but it should be grieved – even by the victorious side (chapter 31, my version):

Weapons are ominous tools.
They are not the noble ruler's tools.
He only uses them when he can't avoid it.
Peace and quiet are preferred.
Victory should not be praised.
Those who praise victory relish manslaughter.

Though he had nothing to say about fighters, he did say something similar to this quote about warriors in chapter 68:

Excellent warriors are not violent.
Excellent soldiers are not furious.

Here is D. C. Lau's version from 1963 (page 130):

One who excels as a warrior does not appear formidable;
One who excels in fighting is never roused in anger.

There is a distinct difference between fighter and fighting. The former delights in it, the latter is not necessarily done with the same sentiment. Lau's version indicates that both lines deal with warriors.

Here is Robert G. Henricks' version from 1989 (page 162):

One who is good at being a warrior doesn't make a show of his might;
One who is good in battle doesn't get angry.

If the quote discussed here is a misinterpretation of something in *Tao Te Ching*, it is most likely the second of these two lines. But the difference between a fighter and a soldier is tremendous. The fighter wants to fight, but the warrior wishes to avoid it, if possible.

Still, for both of them it is true that they should not act out of anger or fury. Otherwise the soldier would be monstrous, causing additional mayhem, and the fighter in a sport would lose control and probably break the rules.

The earliest example I have found of the quote examined here is in a book from 1954: *The faiths men live by*, by the theologian Charles Francis Potter (1885-1962). He claimed to quote Lao Tzu, unfortunately without giving a source. Here is the whole paragraph of that quote (page 79):

The best soldier is not warlike. The best fighter is never angry. The best conqueror takes part in no war. The best employer does not look down but up to his employees. This is the virtue of non-contesting. This is the secret of bringing out other men's ability.

I have not been able to find a *Tao Te Ching* version with that exact wording. I guess Potter allowed himself some paraphrasing, and that might be the reason he did not give any source to this or any other Lao Tzu quote he used in the book. The word "fighter" is not the only odd choice in this quote. So is "employee." Both choices were probably intended to modernize Lao Tzu's words.

Still, it is definitely chapter 68, in its entirety. Here is my version of the whole chapter:

Excellent warriors are not violent.
Excellent soldiers are not furious.
Excellent conquerors do not engage.
Excellent leaders of people lower themselves.

This is called the virtue of no strife.
This is called the use of people's capacity.
This is called the union with Heaven.
It is the perfection of the ancients.

The career of a sage

"The career of a sage is of two kinds:
He is either honored by all in the world,
Like a flower waving its head,
Or else he disappears into the silent forest."

This is not a Lao Tzu quote, but it got one thing right. His ideal for the sage – or for anyone of significance – was to modestly hide from praise, and if he did not he just wasn't much of a sage. Already in chapter 2 of *Tao Te Ching* he stated (my version):

> *So, the sage acts by doing nothing,*
> *Teaches without speaking,*
> *Attends all things without making claim on them,*
> *Works for them without making them dependent,*
> *Demands no honor for his deed.*
> *Because he demands no honor,*
> *He will never be dishonored.*

The quote examined here has some decorative language that does not fit Lao Tzu. But a flower waving its head can be seen as a symbol of parading, which is something he would shun. And disappearing into the silent forest is a sweet symbol of quietude and modesty. So, those are not his words, but also not that far from his meaning.

The word career, on the other hand, is misplaced in a text from at least 2,300 years ago. Its origin must be much nearer to our time, and indeed it is.

The first occurrence of it that I have found is in a book from 1977: *Elegant Sayings*, by the Buddhist philosophers Nāgārjuna and Sakya Pandit (page 8). So, the book is recent, but the two sources are not. Nāgārjuna lived around the 2nd century CE, and Sakya Pandit (usually spelled Pandita) 1182-1251. I found no information about who was the translator. If it is not Tarthang Tulku, it might be Keith Dowman.

The quote discussed here is from Nāgārjuna's *Prajñādaṇḍa* (*The Staff of Wisdom*). The problem is that this text of 260 sayings is very unlikely to be by Nāgārjuna.

Still, the sayings are written in poetic form and have their similarities to *Tao Te Ching* both in style and content. Therefore it is no mystery how this quote has been mistakenly attributed to Lao Tzu somewhere along the way.

None of the few books with the mistaken accreditation is older than 2014, so they are likely to have gotten it from the Internet. In a Google search, the oldest appearance of the quote with an ascertained date is in a blog post from 2011, changing "he" to "she" and ascribing it to Lao Tzu. The same year it started to appear on Facebook.

That is quite late, considering the book is from 1977. There are also web pages with the proper accreditation of the quote to Nāgārjuna, but they are few in comparison. A Google search shows that there are about 230 of those, but well over 4,000 ascribing it to Lao Tzu (August 2020). So it goes.

The flame that burns

"The flame that burns twice as bright burns half as long."

Lao Tzu said nothing about flames or burning in *Tao Te Ching*, but he would approve of the moral of this quote. He even spoke about dimming the light as an ideal, for example in chapter 56 (my version):

Seal the openings.
Shut the doors.
Dull the sharpness.
Untie the knots.
Dim the light.
Become one with the dust.

Also the Way itself, *Tao*, has this trait. Chapter 4 says about it:

It dulls the sharpness,
Unties the knots,
Dims the light,
Becomes one with the dust.

The quote examined here does not only deal with brightness, but warns against overdoing things and being too energetic. Lao Tzu would agree with that as well. It would only wear you down and lead you astray. Chapter 15 states:

He who holds on to the Way seeks no excess.
Since he lacks excess,
He can grow old in no need to be renewed.

So, although Lao Tzu was not the source to this quote he would not object to it. Then, who was?

There are many sayings of this kind. An old and widely familiar one is the expression "burning the candle at both ends" of French origin, introduced to the English language in 1611 by Randle Cotgrave in *A Dictionarie of the French and English Tongues*.

But there is a more recent example, much closer to the quote discussed here. In the 1982 movie *Blade Runner*, the character Dr. Tyrell says to the replicant Roy Batty, when explaining why his life cannot be extended:

The light that burns twice as bright burns half as long –
and you have burned so very, very brightly, Roy.

Amusing as it seems, it is quite plausible that the movie line somehow became a Lao Tzu quote. I have not found any reference to the quote before 1982, neither the "flame" nor the "light" version.

The oldest book I have found to accredit the quote to Lao Tzu is as recent as 2019: *Opium: How an Ancient Flower Shaped and Poisoned Our World*, by John H. Halpern and David Blistein (page 89).

On the Internet, the earliest appearance of the quote ascribed to Lao Tzu was on Goodreads, where it got its first like on August 28, 2008. On Facebook, the first post with the Lao Tzu reference was on January 27, 2010. Both used "flame" instead of "light."

The heart that gives

"The heart that gives, gathers."

The heart as a symbol is in Chinese tradition not the same as it is in the West. We connect it to love and other emotions, whereas the Chinese concept stands for the mind and the will. Lao Tzu also used the word with that connotation several times in *Tao Te Ching*, for example in chapter 8 (my version):

A good mind is deep.

And in the melancholy chapter 20, where Lao Tzu sighed at being alone with his thoughts, as if he were the only one completely mistaken:

I have the mind of a fool,
Understanding nothing.

But he did not use the word in the sense of the quote examined here. It could just as well be expressed as 'kindness brings its own reward' or 'what you give is what you get' and so on. What makes it questionable is the implication that the goal of giving would be what it leads to you receiving. You give, and then you can gather. Like an investment.

To Lao Tzu, as to many other great thinkers of the past, good deeds should be made without any concern of personal gratification. You should be good because it is good, and that should be enough. He wrote in chapter 49:

The sage has no concern for himself,
But makes the concerns of others his own.
He is good to those who are good.
He is also good to those who are not good.
That is the virtue of good.
He is faithful to people who are faithful.
He is also faithful to people who are not faithful.
That is the virtue of faithfulness.

Still, the quote discussed here has often been ascribed to Lao Tzu – but not only to him. Frequently, it is accredited to the American poet Marianne Moore (1887-1972). I searched collections of her writing, but could not find the quote there. It has also been ascribed to the British author Hannah More (1745-1833), but I did not find it when searching through her collected works. This is an elusive quote.

It is also a strange saying. A heart that is giving and gathering is an odd organ, even if it is to be understood symbolically. It would make more sense to say, for example, that a heart finding joy in giving will be pleased by getting. The heart is not doing the job, though it might be the motivator.

Who can be doing the actual giving and gathering, then? The hand, of course. And there is a saying that must be the original form of the quote discussed here:

The hand that gives, gathers.

The oldest record of it I found is in *Paroimiographia* (*Proverbs*) from 1659, by James Howell. The saying is in a chapter of the book on British proverbs, in the section "Other sayings, not unworthy the Consideration."

So, that wording has been with us for long, whereas the version with "heart" is much more recent.

The earliest occurrence I have found of the "heart" version in print is *International Stereotypers' and Electrotypers' Union Journal*, volume 54, from 1959, calling it an old English proverb (page 66). That indicates it was the Howell source misread. It appeared again in 1964, in *Old Lamps and New*, by Ruth Little (page 9), saying nothing about the origin. Little is sometimes accredited with the saying on the web.

The first books ascribing the quote to Lao Tzu are from 2020, but it happened earlier on the Internet. A web page listing "Great Quotes for Nurses" on May 13, 2013, is the earliest I have found with the quote, stating that it is from *Tao Te Ching*.

In November 2016, Richard Branson had the quote in his column at Virgin, also claiming it to be from *Tao Te Ching*. That probably helped to spread the misconception. Another Richard Branson quote of Lao Tzu is discussed in the chapter "Leadership."

As for memes on the web, the ones with this quote seem to be rather equally divided between ascribing Lao Tzu and Marianne Moore. The Goodreads website has the quote twice, ascribing it to Lao Tzu and Marianne Moore respectively. The former got its first like in 2014 and the latter as early as 2008, which was the year after the website launched.

I would put my bet on the quote originating with Howell's *Paroimiographia* and then misquoted with "heart" instead of "hand," much later to be ascribed to Lao Tzu, since the proverb was anonymous to begin with. I still have to figure out how it got ascribed to both Hannah More and Marianne Moore. My guess would be that it started with Hannah as several older books indicate, though I don't know how, and then someone got the wrong Moore for it.

The key to growth

"The key to growth is the introduction of higher dimensions of consciousness into our awareness."

Neither dimensions nor consciousness or awareness are concepts that Lao Tzu would have been comfortable using – or even familiar with. It is a language and reasoning belonging to the last hundred years or so, when psychology was established as a science with its own terminology, and when Asian spiritual traditions were adapted by the Western world, also developing a terminology of its own.

Only if the concepts of this quote are simplified and concretized can it approach Lao Tzu's perspective. Higher dimensions of consciousness would to Lao Tzu be wisdom, awareness would be something like understanding, and growth would be reaching the level of sage. Thereby a sort of similar quote at all possible to be from Lao Tzu would be something like: The sage is wise enough to understand.

But Lao Tzu said neither. He was not much for truisms. Of course the wise will understand – that's the whole point of wisdom. And that the sage is wise is just tautological. The quote discussed here contains the same self-evident reasoning: expanding our awareness makes us grow, at least mentally. Well, duh…

On the Internet, the quote is ascribed to Lao Tzu just about wherever it appears. That is also true for books of the last few years. But in the oldest book I have found with this exact quote, *Toward the One* from 1974 (page 118) by the Sufi

Pir Vilayat Inayat Khan (1916-2004), there is no reference to Lao Tzu or *Tao Te Ching*.

I have not been able to check if the book mentions other references for this quote, but it surely fits Pir Vilayat Inayat Khan's thinking much better than that of Lao Tzu. Also, in the book *Big Vision, Small Business* from 2002, by Jamie S. Walter, the quote is accredited to Pir Vilayat Khan (page 40).

The oldest book I have found ascribing the quote to Lao Tzu is *Self & Spirit* from 2007 (page 304), a collection of quotes edited by Emma Maule. No source is given to the Lao Tzu accreditation. In 2009 the quote and Lao Tzu accreditation might have gotten a wider spread through the book *Drinking with George*, by the actor George Wendt, famous from the TV sitcom *Cheers* (page 1).

In a Google search, the web page with the oldest ascertained date for this quote is in a blog post from August, 2009. It ascribes the quote to Lo Tzu. The first posting of the quote on Facebook is from June 2010, also accrediting Lao Tzu.

It seems that George Wendt had a lot to do with the spread of the false Lao Tzu accreditation. But both he and Maule might have gotten it from the Internet, though I didn't find an occurrence old enough there. The web changes oh, so quickly.

The moment truth is asserted

"The moment truth is asserted it becomes false."

This is a very strange statement, indeed. How can a truth become false when it is asserted? It makes no sense. It was either true or untrue already before being asserted. The claim itself does not make it false. Of course, a claim alone is no proof. Evidence is needed, but when the evidence is there, that's it – until other evidence invalidates it.

There are many reflections through the history of human thought about the difficulty of finding the truth, and what is true to some is blatant lie to others. That is the message of Pontius Pilates' response when Jesus said he came into the world to bear witness to the truth: "What is truth?" (John 18:38).

But a truth does not become untrue because it is asserted. Nor does it become untrue because someone else asserts to it being so. That's just quarreling. In modern terminology we would say that a statement is neither true nor false before being tested, it is but an hypothesis. If it passes the test it is true, if not it is false.

As far as I have found, this quote seems to originate with the Indian guru Bhagwan Shree Rajneesh (1931-1990), later called Osho, who was famous and had many followers in the 1970's and 80's. He mentioned it in a speech on August 19, 1980, accrediting it to Lao Tzu.

That and other speeches were recorded by his disciples and later published in several books, none of them giving the year of publication. The exact date of this speech is given in *Theologia Mystica* by Narinder Sharma (page 139).

In another speech five days earlier, also documented in this book (page 61), Osho had another Lao Tzu quote, which most likely refers to the same saying, though with different wording:

Truth cannot be said. The moment you say it you falsify it.

And in a speech on August 20th, he had this version (page 153):

To say the truth is to falsify it.

Clearly, he was quoting from his own memory and allowing himself to paraphrase. He had a lot of followers for many years, so his version of a Lao Tzu saying has surely spread substantially through the years, leading to the quote examined here being ascribed to Lao Tzu.

Tao Te Ching does not contain such a statement, but Osho was a learned man and probably interpreted some line in the text as he perceived it. My guess is that he based it on the last line of chapter 78, which reads (my version):

True words seem false.

James Legge's version from 1891 reads:

Words that are strictly true seem to be paradoxical.

Lao Tzu didn't question the truth, but stated that it may sound absurd or false to those not understanding it.

He did warn against false claims of knowing the truth,

in several chapters of *Tao Te Ching*. In particular, he distrusted those who took pride in being learned, full of knowledge instead of wisdom, like in the 81st and very last chapter of the book (my version):

True words are not pleasing.
Pleasing words are not true.
Those who are right do not argue.
Those who argue are not right.
Those who know are not learned.
Those who are learned do not know.

It was not that their truth became false upon their announcing it. They were just wrong to begin with.

In the speech where Osho used the quote examined here, he followed up by explaining: "There is no way to communicate truth. But language has to be used; there is no other way. So we always have to use the language with the condition that it cannot be adequate to the experience."

It is close to the nihilistic approach of the Greek philosopher Gorgias, from the 5th century BC, who claimed that nothing exists, and if anything did exist, it could not be known to do so, and finally, if it could be known to exist, this knowledge could not be communicated.

This reasoning is similar to the opening line of *Tao Te Ching*:

The Way that can be walked is not the eternal Way.
The name that can be named is not the eternal name.

D. C. Lau's translation from 1963 of the first line makes the similarity to Osho's thinking even clearer:

The way that can be told is not the constant way.

Lao Tzu said repeatedly in his text that words could not describe *Tao* accurately, and therefore not grasp the fundamental truth of it and its workings. It would not even be possible to come up with an adequate terminology.

So, a plausible expression of Lao Tzu's standpoint regarding the fundamental truth of nature would be something like: A truth that can be stated is not the real truth. That's not so far from the meaning of Osho's quote.

The past has no power

"The past has no power to stop you from being present now. Only your grievance about the past can do that. And what is grievance? The baggage of old thought and emotion."

Being in the now instead of lingering on in the past is a Zen principle. There is that famous anecdote about the old monk carrying a young woman across a river. Later, another monk accompanying him complained about the behavior, not proper for a monk. The old monk replied: "You must be tired, carrying that girl all this way. I put her down as soon as we got to the other side of the river" (*Zen in English Literature and Oriental Classics*, by R. H. Blyth, 1942, page 278).

Living in the now may seem precious, but there are complications. The experience and understanding acquired through life would wash away if we decided to ignore our past. So would the vast fortune of memories that makes us know that we have lived.

If we are to take the principle of living only in the now literally, we might as well be dead. That is particularly true if we denounce "old thought and emotion." They surely contain reasons for grievance, but also for joy and realizations. We would be blank without them, making no progress ever.

The quote examined here hardly survives scrutiny. Nor does it have anything to do with Lao Tzu. Like most Chinese thinkers of old he cherished the past, regarding it as a golden age. Chapter 15 of *Tao Te Ching* starts (my version):

Ancient masters of excellence had a subtle essence,
And a depth too profound to comprehend.

Lao Tzu was sure to share the conviction that we can and should get wiser by age. His name is sort of honorary, with the literary meaning "old child," indicating someone who has made good use of his years since childhood. He would not propagate forgetting all that experience.

Although Lao Tzu is often accredited with the quote, just a simple web search shows that so is another person: Eckhart Tolle, the popular author and speaker on spiritual subjects. He is the origin of the quote, writing the sentences in his book *A New Earth: Awakening to Your Life's Purpose* from 2005 (page 66). They are his own words, he was not quoting anyone.

Tolle was inspired by, among others, Lao Tzu, mentioning him in the book and even quoting from *Tao Te Ching* (using the Feng and English version from 1972 without accrediting that source), which he called "one of the most profound spiritual books ever written" (page 14). But he seems to have drawn even more from Zen, probably also his thoughts in the quote discussed here.

The reason why the universe is eternal

"The reason why the universe is eternal is that it does not live for itself; it gives life to others as it transforms."

The term 'universe' has sometimes been used in translations of *Tao Te Ching*, although it is a concept far from what was imagined in ancient China. A more adequate word for what Lao Tzu meant and perceived is 'world.'

Also, the idea of the universe transforming is something closer to our conception of how it all works than what he might have imagined. He saw there was movement on earth as well as in the sky, but would not describe it as transformation. To him, the world had reached its form at the dawn of its emergence and would remain so forever.

And who are the "others," given life by that transformation? The universe contains everyone and everything, There is no other. It would make more sense to say, for example, that the movements in the world create life within it. That is also how to approach something actually written in *Tao Te Ching*. Chapter 5 states (my version):

> *Is not the space between Heaven and Earth like a bellows?*
> *It is empty, but lacks nothing.*
> *The more it moves, the more comes out of it.*

Heaven and Earth were to Lao Tzu the whole world or, to be more precise, the framework of the world. In between these two opposites was where the continuous process of creation took place. Still, the true creative force was not Heaven and Earth, but that out of which they were formed: Tao, the Way. Already the first chapter makes it clear, calling Tao "the nameless":

The nameless is the beginning of Heaven and Earth.

After having emerged out of *Tao*, Heaven and Earth were established and would last forever, continuously producing new life. Chapter 7 declares:

Heaven is eternal and Earth is lasting.
How can they be eternal and lasting?
Because they do not live for themselves.
That is how they can be eternal.

These lines are most likely the origin of the quote examined here, maybe in combination with the bellows process described in chapter 5.

This somewhat elaborate quote would most likely have an origin, either an odd version of *Tao Te Ching* or a text commenting it. I have not been able to trace it in either. The closest semblance to the quote is in a *Tao Te Ching* version by Jerry O. Dalton from 1993 (page 16 in the 1996 edition):

The universe is eternal.
Why is the universe eternal?
It does not live for itself.
Thus it is everlasting.

Close, but no cigar. It lacks the words in the quote examined here about giving life by transforming, nor is that possible to deduct from his version of chapter 5.

Another quite similar version is that by Lin Yutang from 1948 (page 73):

The universe is everlasting.
The reason the universe is everlasting
Is that it does not live for Self.
Therefore it can long endure.

The word "Self" is confusing, but Yutang explained it in a footnote: "Gives life to others through its transformations." So, there is the transforming. Also, Yutang's wording of the lines from chapter 5 would bring some support to the quote examined here (page 63):

How the universe is like a bellows!
Empty, yet it gives a supply that never fails;
The more it is worked, the more it brings forth.

It is difficult to decide if the quote is paraphrased from Yutang or Dalton, or a combination thereof, but at least they indicate how the quote might have been formed.

The earliest book I have found with the exact quote is *The Celestial Fortune Cookie: An Astrological Book of Days with Quotations for Every Sign* from 2000, by Andrea Valeria. The quote was accredited to Lao Tzu and assigned to the Zodiac sign Sagittarius (page 426). Valeria used several quotes, mostly accrediting them to Lao Tzu but a few times to *Tao Te Ching*. It seems that she used different sources, maybe from the Internet in those rather early days of it.

The Internet gives no clue to the origin of the quote. I have found no ascertained earlier appearance on the web than 2011. On Goodreads, the quote got its first like on June 8, 2011. Also on Facebook, the quote started to appear in 2011, the first two actually on January 8, which is before the first Goodreads like. Probably, the one got the other started. They all accredited Lao Tzu, but without giving any source.

Since the quote had kind of a little boom on the web in 2011, the reason is probably not Valeria's book from 2000, nor the three books from 2007 and 2008 with the quote: *Law of attraction* by David Hooper (page 28), *Java data mining* by Hornick et al (page 451), and *One reckless summer* by Toni Blake (page 153). But the one to come next, *From Eternity to Here: The Quest for the Ultimate Theory of Time* from 2010, by Sean Carroll (page 82), was just in time to create some Internet noise the following year.

On the other hand, Carroll and others might have found the quote on an older web site that I have not been able to find.

Of the books mentioned above, only Hooper's gives a source to the quote: *The Tao Te Ching of Lao Tzu* from 2001, by Brian Browne Walker. Unfortunately, I have not found the quote in that source, nor did I find a 2001 edition. The book was initially published in 1995 and 1996, with a new edition in 2011. Well, 2001 can just be a reprint. None of the other editions contains the quote.

If it is simply a typo, it has been persistent. Hooper's book has three Lao Tzu quotes, all given the same source, and I could find none of them there. Nor did I find it in Walker's version of *Hua Hu Ching*, falsely claimed to contain Lao Tzu's words. Instead, one is a Chuang Tzu quote in Arthur Waley's 1934 version of *Tao Te Ching*, discussed in the chapter "To a mind that is still" of this book, and the other is from *Poems of the Universe: Lao Tzu's Tao Te Ching* from 2005, by Brian Donohue (page 40), which seems only to exist as a PDF file on the web. None of those books contains the quote examined here, though. Nor did I find any book with all three quotes, so the origin of the quote examined here remains hidden.

The snow goose need not bathe

"The snow goose need not bathe to make itself white. Neither need you do anything but be yourself."

This quote is easy enough to understand. It is about nature already providing us with all we need, similar to what Jesus said about the lilies in Matthew 6:28-29 (King James Version):

> *And why take ye thought for raiment? Consider the lilies of the field, how they grow; they toil not, neither do they spin:*
> *And yet I say unto you, that even Solomon in all his glory was not arrayed like one of these.*

But Lao Tzu never mentioned the snow goose in *Tao Te Ching*. He did not even mention either snow or geese. So, how this maxim got connected to Lao Tzu is bewildering.

He would also reject the idea of being yourself, wondering how being anything else could be at all possible. He did, however, recommend modesty in all, even for the high and mighty. In chapter 39 he stated (my version):

> *The noble must make humility his root.*
> *The high must make the low its base.*

He ended the chapter with this advice:

So, do not strive for the shine of jade,
But clatter like stone.

The oldest book in which I have found the complete quote examined here is *The Mystic Path to Cosmic Power* from 1967, by Vernon Howard. He accredited it to *Tao*, by which he might have meant Lao Tzu or Chuang Tzu (page 113), who were both mentioned on the previous page. His vague reference implies that he was paraphrasing, in spite of using quotes.

The next book to contain the quote is *A Guide for the Advanced Soul* from 1984, by Susan Hayward, where it is accredited to Lao Tzu (the book lacks pagination). And then *You'll See It when You Believe It* from 1989, by Wayne W. Dyer, also claiming it to be from Lao Tzu (page 155). Other books have followed, with the same accreditation. None gives any reference to a *Tao Te Ching* version, or even what chapter it would be from.

There is, though, a similar saying in the book of Chuang Tzu, which reads in James Legge's *Texts of Taoism*, volume 1, from 1891 (page 357):

The snow-goose does not bathe every day to make itself white, nor the crow blacken itself every day to make itself black.

That is from the 14th book of Chuang Tzu, called "The Revolution of Heaven." The 14th book belongs to the group called the "Outer Chapters," which are considered not to be Chuang Tzu's own words. The text claims that the quote was from Lao Tzu's mouth, which should be doubted even more.

In any case, this Chuang Tzu quote must be the origin of the quote examined here. It does not say you should just be yourself, but something that could very well be interpreted that way. The Chuang Tzu text continues:

> *The natural simplicity of their black and white does not afford any ground for controversy; and the fame and praise which men like to contemplate do not make them greater than they naturally are.*

Although wordier, I still prefer the Chuang Tzu version. Anyway, neither version of the quote is from *Tao Te Ching*, and was most likely never uttered by Lao Tzu.

The soul has no secret

"The soul has no secret that the behavior does not reveal."

The soul as we see it is not a concept with which Lao Tzu would be familiar. When we speak of the soul, we incorporate ideas of a Christian tradition, suggesting among other things something separate from the body — maybe even surviving it. Lao Tzu did not express a belief in an afterlife or anything in man separable from his body.

Well, we use 'soul' for so many different things relating to the human mind and awareness. So, it is possible to use it, carefully, in the translation of an ancient Chinese text. I have done so in my version of *Tao Te Ching*, at the start of Chapter 10:

> *Can you make your soul embrace the One*
> *And not lose it?*

Where my interpretation and many others write 'soul,' the Chinese text speaks of two concepts that should be combined: *ying* and *p'o*. They are difficult to translate, but suggest two sides of the human mind: spiritual and physical. A daring comparison, somewhat doubtful, would be consciousness and instinct. But that's stretching it. Anyway, what Lao Tzu referred to was the human mind as a whole, its parts combined.

Writing this, I'm starting to think I should have used another word than soul in my translation — if I could just find the accurate one.

The same goes for behavior. This broad term could also be used, though carefully, in a translation of Lao Tzu's *Tao Te Ching*.

Still, the main problem with this fake Lao Tzu quote is that it points to the psyche of an individual personality, which is far from how Lao Tzu regarded mankind. It's a modern view of the mind as something internal, hidden from the minds of others and using this secrecy to get ahead.

To Lao Tzu, human beings were basically the same, and so was their mentality. Some got wiser and thereby acted nobly, in accordance with *Tao*, the Way. The others were driven by basic needs and urges that were far from secret.

The idea that anyone would try to hide and even fake his personality was alien to Lao Tzu. He did not even say something that suggested people have personalities different from those of others. To him, we are all pretty much the same. The differences are in what we understand, not what we strive to be.

He did see actions, which can be translated to behavior, as what revealed the wisdom acquired. The wise would act according to their wisdom, as would the unwise according to their lack of it. Pretense had nothing to do with it, since they could do nothing else.

I haven't found a *Tao Te Ching* version containing the quote examined here. Nor did I find it in a Google book search. It seems to have appeared on the Internet.

A Facebook search finds the first appearance of the fake quote on October 17, 2013, giving neither Lao Tzu nor anyone else as the source. It didn't reappear on Facebook until 2016, where it got accredited to Lao Tzu.

There is, though, a similar quote:

The soul has no secrets which the conduct will not reveal.

This wording has quite another background. I found it in *A Dictionary of Quotations in Most Frequent Use*, by David Evans Macdonnel, published 1803 (4th edition, 1st edition 1799). According to the author, it's a Chinese proverb he translated from its French version: "L'âme n'a point de secret que la conduite ne révèle."

The French wording can be found in *Abrégé du Journal de Paris*, p. 359, where it is also explained as a Chinese proverb (*maxime*). The book was printed in Paris 1789 — a year of revolutionary significance in that city. But the quote is from a 1777 article of the Journal.

It is not difficult to see how a Chinese proverb becomes accredited to the most legendary of Chinese philosophers. But Lao Tzu said nothing of the kind.

The way to do

"The way to do is to be."

What way this quote ascribed to Lao Tzu comments is hardly the Way of which he spoke. It is rather nonsensical, like a joking wordplay. That is also what it has become, in a famous threesome that appeared at first as graffiti on a warehouse wall in Richardson, Texas. A Dallas newspaper reported in January 1968:

> Bud Crew says that a month ago he wrote this on the warehouse wall at Bud's Tool Cribs in Richardson: "'The way to do is to be.' — Leo-tzu, Chinese philosopher."
> A few days later, a salesman wrote under that: "'The way to be is to do.' — Dale Carnegie,"
> Recently, says Crew, an anonymous sage has added still another axiom: "'Do be, do be, do.' — Frank Sinatra."

My source is the website Quote Investigator in a text from 2013 (quoteinvestigator.com/2013/09/16/do-be-do/). I don't know if the misspelling of Lao Tzu's name was on that wall or in the newspaper only.

It is hard to make serious sense of the quote. Lao Tzu preached non-action, *wu-wei*, so he would recommend just being instead of hurrying to do things. But it would not work as a complete substitute. There are still things needed to be done in our daily lives. Nor is 'being' to Lao Tzu a state of its own, a sufficient form of human existence. That's more Zen, at least symbolically. He would rather have it something like: We are what we do, so we have to be careful about what we do. Not that he said those words, either.

Still, this quote is from a *Tao Te Ching* version, by Witter Bynner in 1944. It's the last line of chapter 47 (page 55 in the 1962 edition). Bynner was so fond of it that he also wrote it on a page of its own in the beginning of the book, as if this quote were the essence of Lao Tzu's teaching.

But it is a questionable translation of that line in *Tao Te Ching*. It is the third of characteristics of the sage (my version):

Completes without acting.

James Legge in 1891 expressed it, about the sages (page 89):

...accomplished their ends without any purpose of doing so.

It is the *wu-wei* method of fixing things with minimal interference, which is not the same as simply being. To Lao Tzu, total passivity was no goal in itself, but by not springing into hasty action many additional problems would be avoided. Given time, things tend to solve themselves.

Bynner's big portion of poetic license, so to speak, is increased by his use of rhymes. That certainly does not make translating *Tao Te Ching* easier, if trying to stay close to the original content. But it's not an unreasonable aspiration.

The major part of Lao Tzu's text is written in rhymes. Bernhard Karlgren (1889-1978) in an essay on the subject from 1932 found that about three quarters of *Tao Te Ching* are in verse (page 4). But that is so much easier in Chinese, since there are many words sounding the same. Furthermore, the Chinese tradition allows for rhyming with the same word. Most other languages lack these benefits, which is why few translators have made the same choice. When they have done so, it has been only with sections rhymed in the Chinese text. So did James Legge, but not with this chapter.

Not only with the rhyming, Bynner allowed himself significant deviations from the original, especially regarding the last three lines:

Search your heart and see
If he is wise who takes each turn:
The way to do is to be.

I would say that he got caught by his rhymes. Here is my wording:

The sage knows without traveling,
Perceives without looking,
Completes without acting.

Legge wrote, with an explanatory remark within parentheses:

Therefore the sages got their knowledge without travelling; gave their (right) names to things without seeing them; and accomplished their ends without any purpose of doing so.

For more about Witter Bynner and his version of *Tao Te Ching*, see the chapter "A man with outward courage."

There are many paths

"There are many paths to enlightenment. Be sure to take the one with a heart."

This fake Lao Tzu quote is so banal, I hesitate even to include it. Paths don't have hearts. It would make more sense to say "choose with your heart." And if so, shouldn't we choose paths with our hearts, whether they lead to enlightenment or not?

Of course, enlightenment is a Buddhist concept, not Taoist. Within Zen, the Japanese word *satori* is usually translated enlightenment. It refers to a sudden experience of insight and clarity.

Then there is the Enlightenment of European thought in the 18th century, but I bet that's not intended in the quote.

Lao Tzu said nothing about enlightenment or a sudden burst of understanding, like a moment of revelation. He spoke more about wisdom, something attained from contemplating over time and following *Tao*, the Way.

Also the idea of following one's heart is alien to Lao Tzu and his time. The heart as an organ of compassion and emotions is a Western idea. The heart is more a symbol of the mind and will-power in the Far East.

Yet another absurdity with the quote is the idea of many paths. *Tao*, the Way, can also be translated the Path – and Lao Tzu would revolt against the idea of more than one *Tao*, or that it would at all be possible to choose another one than the *Tao* he spoke about. To him, there was one Way, and the whole world without exception was ruled by it.

This fake Lao Tzu quote is so off, and so conventional, its originator can be just about anyone. Not much thought was needed to come up with it. I'd even say that evidently not much thought was put into it.

The quote has been around, falsely accredited to Lao Tzu, for longer than the Internet. I found it in *Treasury of Spiritual Wisdom* from 1996 by Andy Zubko (page 128), a book also mentioned in the chapter "Life and death are one thread." It contains several Lao Tzu quotes that must be deemed fake, with no mention of a source or reference to a chapter of *Tao Te Ching*. So, I don't know where he got this and some other questionable Lao Tzu quotes.

It is quite likely that a lot of later occurrences of this quote stem from his book. For more about its Lao Tzu quotes, see the chapter "Life and death are one thread."

There are similar expressions leading to other sources, but none of them to Lao Tzu. The book *Spiritual Growth* from 1989, by Sanaya Roman, states the following (page 12):

There are many paths to enlightenment. Choose the path that is most joyful to you and in alignment with your values.

Another candidate as origin of the quote examined here is Deepak Chopra. The book *Examining alternative medicine* from 2001, by Paul C. Reisser, quotes from an "Ask Deepak" section of his website (page 195):

There are many paths to enlightenment ... listen to your heart and choose which one feels best for you.

Reisser gave the date for this quote as May 23, 1998, but that section has since been removed from the website. It remains on Internet Archive, though, where the full quote reads: "There are many paths to enlightenment, which can include love of a fellow human being, love of a guru or love of the Divine. Listen to your heart and choose which one feels best for you."

The Chopra wording is much nearer than Roman's to that of the quote examined here. But it is from 1998, when Zubko's book had already been around for two years. If Chopra had made the same statement in one of his many books, it would probably have come up in my Google Books and Internet Archive searches, but it did not.

Andy Zubko's book remains the most probable first source to the quote, and he might have paraphrased a Buddhist saying.

There is a time to live

"There is a time to live and a time to die, but never to reject the moment."

Though accredited with this quote, Lao Tzu would insist that there is no specific time to live, but a way to do it – following *Tao*, the Way. That is all. Those who did not follow *Tao* were prone to rush through life, as stated in the beginning of chapter 50 of *Tao Te Ching* (my version):

> *We go from birth to death.*
> *Three out of ten follow life.*
> *Three out of ten follow death.*
> *People who rush from birth to death*
> *Are also three out of ten.*
> *Why is that so?*
> *Because they want to make too much of life.*

Lao Tzu also pondered the afterlife, but not in the conventional meaning. He wrote in chapter 33:

> *Those who die without being forgotten get longevity.*

This line was for long misunderstood to imply there was something one could do to extend one's life far beyond the normal expectancy. The line was interpreted much like James Legge did in 1891:

> *He who dies and yet does not perish, has longevity.*

But the wording of the two Mawangdui manuscripts from around 200 BC, discovered in the 1970's, made it clear that the long life was in other people's memories, and nowhere else.

This says the same as the old Norse proverb in *Havamal*, here in the 1875 translation by Rasmus Björn Anderson in *Norse Mythology: The Religion of our Forefathers* (page 143):

Cattle die,
Kindred die,
We ourselves also die;
But I know one thing
That never dies, —
Judgment on each one dead.

As for rejecting the moment, Lao Tzu would find it preposterous. How to do that? The moment is a quickly fleeing thing. He was clear about the folly of trying to resist how the world works, but that must be a process over time and not just a single moment. A moment is gone and immediately replaced by another. There is not much sense in pondering it. The word *Tao*, the Way, indicates that there is instead a direction and progression to consider.

The first part of this quote, about a time to live and another to die, is not unknown in the history of thought. It can be found already in the Bible. The beginning of chapter 3 of *Ecclesiastes* reads (King James Version):

To every thing there is a season, and a time to every purpose under the heaven:
A time to be born, and a time to die; a time to plant, and a time to pluck up that which is planted;
A time to kill, and a time to heal; a time to break down,

and a time to build up;
A time to weep, and a time to laugh; a time to mourn, and a time to dance;
A time to cast away stones, and a time to gather stones together; a time to embrace, and a time to refrain from embracing;
A time to get, and a time to lose; a time to keep, and a time to cast away;
A time to rend, and a time to sew; a time to keep silence, and a time to speak;
A time to love, and a time to hate; a time of war, and a time of peace.

This part was used in the Pete Seeger song "Turn! Turn! Turn!," which became a hit with the Byrds in 1965. The chapter ends:

All go unto one place; all are of the dust, and all turn to dust again.
Who knoweth the spirit of man that goeth upward, and the spirit of the beast that goeth downward to the earth? Wherefore I perceive that there is nothing better, than that a man should rejoice in his own works; for that is his portion: for who shall bring him to see what shall be after him?

It is not that far from what *Havamal* states about the matter.

Another interesting perspective on the time for living and dying comes from the English politician Sir Henry Vane (1613-1662), quoted in *The life and death of Sir Henry Vane, Kt.*, by George Sikes, from 1662 — the same year Sir Henry was executed for having collaborated with Oliver Cromwell (page 122):

There is a time to Live and a time to die. A good Death is far better and more eligible than an ill Life. A wise man Lives but so long as his Life is more worth than his Death.

Sadly, Sir Henry was not allowed to make that decision for himself.

The Roman emperor Marcus Aurelius (121-180 CE) had a somewhat similar take on the topic in *Meditations*, here in George Long's translation from 1874 (page 108):

Since it is possible that thou mayest depart from life this very moment, regulate every act and thought accordingly.

As for the quote examined in this chapter, I have not found any book containing it with the exact same wording. The closest thing to it is in Stephen Mitchell's 1988 *Tao Te Ching* version's beginning of chapter 50, to which I gave my version above. Here are his words for the same lines:

*The Master gives himself up
to whatever the moment brings.
He knows that he is going to die,
and he has nothing left to hold on to:
no illusions in his mind,
no resistances in his body.*

As so often, Mitchell allowed himself a substantial portion of freedom from the original text and its content. For more about Stephen Mitchell and his version of *Tao Te Ching*, see the chapter "A good traveler has no fixed plans." Still, his version of chapter 50 is not likely to be the source of the quote. It deviates too much in form, though implying sort of the same meaning.

The quote is much more likely to be derived partly from the famous expression in *Ecclesiastes*, with an addition of its second part from someone with kind of a Zen mind. Its essential message is simply: live in the moment.

It can be compared to another fake Lao Tzu quote discussed in this book: "If you are depressed, you are living in the past. If you are anxious, you are living in the future. If you are at peace, you are living in the moment."

A Google search of the web indicates that the quote discussed here appeared in 2013, but its reappearance was scarce the following years. The spread seems mainly to be by memes, accrediting Lao Tzu. On Facebook, the quote popped up the year before, in November 2012. It was as a cat photo meme, ascribing the quote to Lao Tzu. The meme image file is actually slightly older, from September 18, 2012, so it was probably picked up from somewhere else. Unfortunately, I have not been able to find where.

There is no illusion

"There is no illusion greater than fear."

Lao Tzu did not mention illusion in *Tao Te Ching*. It would be a strange concept to him. Certainly, what he observed about the nature of existence seemed to be hidden from the minds of others, but not really replaced by some illusion. It was a question of seeing what was hidden, which is not the same thing as imagining something else.

But he did speak about fear – not as an illusion, but a real thing for real reasons. For example, in chapter 13 (my version):

What does it mean that praise and disgrace cause fear?
Praise leads to weakness.
Getting it causes fear, losing it causes fear.
This is why praise and disgrace cause fear.

In chapter 17 he mentioned that lesser rulers are feared, and in chapter 74 he even pointed out fear as something to keep people obedient:

If people are not afraid of dying,
Why threaten them with death?
If people live in constant fear of death,
And if breaking the law is punished by death,
Then who would dare?

That was no defense of capital punishment. In the following lines Lao Tzu explained that there is one supreme executioner and it would be a mistake to try taking that place. This executioner is nature, of course, killing each of us at the end.

Lao Tzu did not regard fear as an illusion, but warned about its consequences.

The earliest book in which I have found the exact quote examined here is *Who Am I without You? 52 Ways to Rebuild Self-Esteem after a Breakup* from 2015, by Christina G. Hibbert. The quote, ascribed to Lao Tzu, commences a chapter called "Face your fears."

On the Internet the quote has been around for a little longer. It got its first like on Goodreads in January 2013 and its first post on Facebook in December that year, in both cases ascribed to Lao Tzu.

But the same quote with "greater" and "illusion" switching places is found in Stephen Mitchell's version of *Tao Te Ching*, released in 1988. It is in chapter 46:

There is no greater illusion than fear,
no greater wrong than preparing to defend yourself,
no greater misfortune than having an enemy.

Whoever can see through all fear
will always be safe.

As often with Mitchell's version, this wording is far from most translations of *Tao Te Ching*. Here is my version of the same lines:

There is no greater crime than desire.
There is no greater disaster than discontent.
There is no greater misfortune than greed.

Therefore:
To have enough of enough is always enough.

Here is D. C. Lau's wording from 1963 (page 107):

There is no crime greater than having too many desires;
There is no disaster greater than not being content;
There is no misfortune greater than being covetous.
Hence in being content, one will always have enough.

So, it is not about fear at all. Mitchell has gone his own way, and I don't understand how he got there. Anyway, I bet that Mitchell is the origin of the quote examined here, although with two words switching places.

Oddly, the exact Mitchell quote has not reached nearly as much attention. On Goodreads, Mitchell's wording was not introduced until 2016 and has still received just three likes, compared to 113 for the wording examined here (August 2020). In a Google search, the former brings less than 5,000 links, while the latter brings more than 23,000.

A Google Books search, on the other hand, gives twice the number of results for Mitchell's wording than the other one. That's an argument for trusting books more than the web, I guess.

For more about Stephen Mitchell and his version of *Tao Te Ching*, see the chapter "A good traveler has no fixed plans."

Time is a created thing

"Time is a created thing. To say 'I don't have time,' is like saying, 'I don't want to.'"

Lao Tzu did not contemplate time as such. Nothing in his writing suggests that he thought of it as being relative or a chimera. He most probably regarded it as an eternal absolute. In chapter 25 he described *Tao*, the Way, as preceding the world – but not preceding time itself. Here it is in my version:

> There was something that finished chaos,
> Born before Heaven and Earth.
> So silent and still!
> So pure and deep!
> It stands alone and immutable,
> Ever-present and inexhaustible.
> It can be called the mother of the whole world.
> I do not know its name. I call it the Way.
> For the lack of better words I call it great.

The idea of time as a created thing was suggested by Saint Augustine (354-430 CE), but he meant that time was created by God in the commencement of his world creation – not something that mere humans could make up their own minds about. To Augustine it was an argument against questions about what was before the world, or for that matter before God: There was no before, since he started time when he created the world.

He wrote in *Confessions*, book XI (revised from a former translation by F. B. Pusey in 1838, page 234):

For that very time didst Thou make, nor could times pass by, before Thou madest those times. But if before heaven and earth there was no time, why is it demanded, what Thou then didst? For there was no "then," when there was no time.

This perspective from 1,600 years ago is remarkably comparable to the modern Big Bang theory, which states that time, as we know it, started when the universe started to expand.

But this is very far from the time concept suggested by the quote discussed here, which deals with a personal relation to time – the time one has, and how one chooses to spend it. That perspective is not cosmological, but moral.

The earliest printed book I have found with the precise quote examined here accredited to Lao Tzu is *La Vida Rica: The Latina's Guide to Success* from 2004, by Yrma Rico and Nancy Garascia (page 73). But the previous year another book was published, accrediting it to someone else: *Soul Sex Tantra for Two* from 2003, by Pala Copeland and Al Link (page 22). They ascribed the quote to the Christian author Elisabeth 'Betty' Elliot (1926-2015).

Apart from plenty of accreditations to Lao Tzu, the quote has more than once been accredited to Betty Elliot, who famously spent two years as a missionary with an Ecuadorian tribe that had previously killed her husband. Although she did not express it exactly like the quote discussed here, it is close enough to determine that she is the source to it, though slightly paraphrased. It is in her book *Discipline: The Glad Surrender* from 1982, with a paperback edition in 2006 (page 93):

> *Time is a creature – a created thing – and a gift. We cannot make any more of it. We can only receive it and be faithful stewards in the use of it.*
> *"I don't have time" is probably a lie more often than not, covering "I don't want to." We have time – twenty-four hours in a day, seven days in a week.*

Like Augustine, she insisted that time was created by God, and each person's time on earth is decided by the same entity. So, she preached that we should treat the time we are given with gratitude and make good use of it.

The paraphrasing in the quote is misleading also about her thoughts, since it implies that time would be something we invent to excuse our own unwillingness to do our duties. In other words, neither Lao Tzu nor Betty Elliot would agree on it.

To a mind that is still

"To a mind that is still the whole universe surrenders."

Some Internet posts and memes write "the mind" instead of "a mind," which makes no difference to the meaning.

The idea that the universe should surrender to a human mind would be absurd to Lao Tzu. On the contrary, humankind must yield to the Way of Heaven and learn its working in order to adapt to it. Nonetheless, the main method by which we can reach this awareness and accept it is by stillness, *wu-wei* (non-action), and by letting the world take its course.

Also, the term "universe" is questionable when translating Lao Tzu, since it has a meaning today so far from the understanding of ancient times. In Lao Tzu's China the whole world was one of Heaven and Earth – and the ten thousand things, which simply meant everything in between those two. So, the most adequate word for it all would be the world. Still, several translators have used the word "universe," so it is sort of a matter of taste.

But a surrendering universe won't do.

Still, this is a genuine quote – though from Chuang Tzu, and not Lao Tzu. The mix-up is understandable, since the quote is in Arthur Waley's introduction to his translation of *Tao Te Ching* from 1934 (page 58). He put "still" within quotation marks to signal the complexity of the original Chinese term – and he accredited it to Chuang Tzu, book XIII.1.

He did not state what translation of Chuang Tzu it was from, so probably it was his own. It deviates rather significantly from other versions of the Chuang Tzu text. The version by Herbert A. Giles from 1889 reads (page 158):

The mind of the Sage being in repose becomes the mirror of the universe, the speculum of all creation.

James Legge's version in *Text of Taoism*, volume 1, from 1891 reads (page 331):

The still mind of the sage is the mirror of heaven and earth, the glass of all things.

And here is Burton Watson's version from 1968:

The sage's mind in stillness is the mirror of Heaven and earth, the glass of the ten thousand things.

So, nothing about a surrendering universe. And again, not Lao Tzu.

Occasionally this quote has been ascribed to Lieh Tzu, a 5th century BC philosopher, but the text with his name is considered to be from the 4th century CE. The oldest book with the Lieh Tzu accreditation is *The Tao of Painting* from 1956, by Mai-mai Sze (page 18), giving the same Waley source page as mentioned above, which points to Chuang Tzu and none else.

On this page of Waley's book, he referred the quote to Chuang Tzu in one footnote, and the following note has a reference to Lieh Tzu – but that does not concern this quote. Sze might have mixed that up.

The slightly altered version of the quote, with "the mind" instead of "a mind," may have originated with *The*

Religions of Man from 1958, by Huston Smith (page 180), where the quote from Waley's book was used but with this little typo. This wording is also used in the oldest book I have found to accredit Lao Tzu with the quote: *Zen and the Art of Gardening* from 2000, by Gill Hale (page 217). Several books followed, doing the same.

On the Internet, the false Lao Tzu accreditation has also been around for quite long. On Goodreads the exact quote examined here got its first like January 26, 2008, which was the year after the site was launched. On Facebook the quote started to appear in 2011, but only with Chuang Tzu accreditations. It took until May 2014 for the first post ascribing it to Lao Tzu to appear, with an accompanying meme.

The version with "the mind," though, appeared in 2010, already then with the Lao Tzu accreditation. In books as well as on the web, it seems that most Lao Tzu references are with "the mind" and most Chuang Tzu references with "a mind."

To hold

"To hold, you must first open your hand. Let go."

Indeed, if you want to grab something you must start with an open hand. A fist can hold on to nothing. The paradox is in "let go." So you hold on just to let go? Well, it is the only way to get hold of something else. Still, this is a strange message. It seems to say: always let go, so that you can hold anew. Perpetuum mobile.

Letting go, though, was something Lao Tzu felt strongly about and recommended as a basic principle of reaching *wu-wei*, non-action. Chapter 48 of *Tao Te Ching* says (my version):

Those who seek the Way,
Let go of something every day.

They let go and let go,
Until reaching no action.
When nothing is done,
Nothing is left undone.

The quote examined here is not from Lao Tzu. He would not regard letting go as something by which to grab something else. Still, it is inspired by his teaching.

The source to this quote is not from the Far East but from 'far out.' It can be found in *Psychedelic Monograph II* from 1966, with a new edition called *Psychedelic Prayers and Other Meditations* in 1997, by the psychologist, writer, and psychedelic drug enthusiast Timothy Leary (1920-1996). The book consists of "psychedelic prayers" based on the first 37 chapters of *Tao Te Ching*. In the foreword, Leary described the Chinese classic as a "psychedelic manual" and *Tao* as an "energy process" (page 37).

The quote is part of a poem called "Take In – Let Go." The whole poem reads (page 64):

To breathe in
You must first breathe out
Let go

To hold
You must first open your hand
Let go

To be warm
You must first be naked
Let go

In an endnote, Leary specified that this poem was adapted from chapter 36 of *Tao Te Ching* (page 134). There is another poem based on the same chapter, called "The Lesson of Seed" (page 79):

The soft overcomes the hard
The small overcomes the large
The gentle survives the strong
The invisible survives the visible

Fish should be left in deep water
Fire and iron kept under ground
Seed should be left free
To grow in the rhythm of life

His interpretations of the chapter are not impossible to extract from the original, though partly deviating from it by the obvious use of poetic license – and admittedly of meditation as well as psychedelic drugs (page 38). Here is my version of the same chapter:

What should be shrunken must first be stretched.
What should be weakened must first be strengthened.
What should be abolished must first be cherished.
What should be deprived must first be enriched.

This is called understanding the hidden.
The soft and weak overcome the hard and strong.

The fish cannot leave the deep waters.
The state's weaponry should not be displayed.

It is understandable how Leary's poems adapted from *Tao Te Ching* chapters were later mistaken to be proper translations of them. After all, many versions claiming to be translations allow themselves even greater liberties with the original than Leary did.

On Goodreads, the quote examined here, ascribed to Lao Tzu, got its first like in November, 2008, which was the year after the website was launched. With that exception, the oldest web page I found with an ascertained date, containing the quote, is from October 2010, also ascribing it to Lao Tzu. On Facebook, the quote seems to have started to appear in 2012.

To see things in the seed

"To see things in the seed, that is genius."

Lao Tzu made no mention of either seed or genius in *Tao Te Ching*. The former is a word he might have used, but certainly not the latter. He spoke of the sage, who had an understanding of *Tao*, the Way. Although he knew that few understood it, he had no doubt they would be able to if they just listened. He wrote in chapter 70 (my version):

> *My words are very easy to understand*
> *And very easy to practice.*
> *Still, no one in the world*
> *Can understand or practice them.*

It was not that they needed to be geniuses to understand. It was more like they just did not care, or their minds were too full of misconceptions.

The term genius and what it stands for today is something developed in the 18th and 19th centuries. It points to an intellectual capacity that someone is born with, not accessible to others by no matter how much schooling. It was not a concept relevant to Lao Tzu, should he have been familiar with it.

So, this is not a Lao Tzu quote, but it is very likely inspired by something he wrote – chapter 64 in *Tao Te Ching*. Its beginning reads:

Stillness is easy to maintain.
What has not yet emerged is easy to prevent.
The brittle is easy to shatter.
The small is easy to scatter.
Solve it before it happens.
Order it before chaos emerges.

Lao Tzu pointed out that even the biggest problem is small in the beginning. But if left unsolved for long, it grows into something that finally risks being insoluble. He mentioned the same in chapter 63:

Meet the difficult while it is easy.
Meet the big while it is small.

It doesn't take a genius to understand that. The trick is to recognize the problem when it is so small that it is hardly a problem at all.

This crux is well known also outside ancient China. There is an expression in English with the same message: to nip something in the bud. It was first recorded in 1606 in the play *The Woman Hater*, by Francis Beaumont and John Fletcher, published in 1607. In act 3, scene 1, the character Oriana says:

I doe confess I am to easie, too much woman,
Not coy enough to take affection,
Yet I can frowne and nip a passion
Euen in the bud.

She might not speak of the kinds of problems Lao Tzu treats, but the solution is the same.

The oldest book I have found to contain the exact quote examined here is *Creative Innovators* from 1988, compiled by Dottie Walters, accrediting it to Lao Tzu (page 273). The book contains one more Lao Tzu quote, equally dubious (page 112): "Knowing others is wisdom, knowing the self is enlightenment." That quote is discussed in the chapter "Knowing others."

One year earlier, though, a variation of the quote, beginning "if you can" instead of just "to," was published in *Movers, Shakers, and Change Makers*, by John Patrick Dolan (page 272). It gives Lao Tzu (spelled Lao Tsze) as the origin, mistakenly adding that he was the mentor of Confucius. I have not found the quote worded like that elsewhere.

There is another version of the quote floating around, with a shorter wording:

To see things in the seed is genius.

The oldest book with that version of the quote is *From Ordinary to Extraordinary* from 1990, by Shall Sinha (page 141), also ascribing it to Lao Tzu. So are most, if not all, web pages with the quote.

On the web, the quote started to appear a couple of years into this millennium – always, as far as I have seen, ascribing it to Lao Tzu and never giving a source for it.

I have not found any older source to the quote than the books from 1987 and 1988 mentioned above, though I suspect there is one somewhere. If this is not a quote from someone else, mistakenly accredited to Lao Tzu, it is probably a very short interpretation of chapter 63 or 64 in *Tao Te Ching*.

To understand the limitation

"To understand the limitation of things, desire them."

This sentence has the wit reminding of Oscar Wilde. Not that he had anything against desire. In his play *Lady Windermere's Fan* from 1892 he had the character Lord Darlington declare (act I): "I can resist everything except temptation." Later in the play, Dumby also has something to say on the subject (act III):

> *In this world there are only two tragedies. One is not getting what one wants, and the other is getting it. The last is much the worst, the last is a real tragedy!*

To Oscar Wilde, desire was a trap with no escape. In his only novel *The Picture of Dorian Gray* from 1891, Lord Henry explains to Dorian (chapter II, page 27):

> *The only way to get rid of a temptation is to yield to it. Resist it, and your soul grows sick with longing for the things it has forbidden to itself, with desire for what its monstrous laws have made monstrous and unlawful.*

Lao Tzu, too, warned against letting desire command us. In chapter 19 of *Tao Te Ching* he said that we should "lessen selfishness and restrain desires" and in chapter 37 he stated (my version):

Without desire there is stillness,
And the world settles by itself.

He did not use the wording of the quote discussed here, but he was aware of the paradox it expresses. To realize how shallow the things that we desire are, we need to examine our desires. He explained it already in the first chapter of *Tao Te Ching*:

Free from desire you see the mystery.
Full of desire you see the manifestations.
These two have the same origin but differ in name.
That is the secret,
The secret of secrets,
The gate to all mysteries.

The mystery he spoke of was the working of *Tao*, the Way, hidden beneath everything in the world and still ruling it. That is only perceivable if we do not allow desires to blind our eyes. Otherwise we only see the result of the Way's workings – the world and everything in it. We see the surface but not the substance.

But then he added that they merely differ in name. We need to observe both to reveal the secret. That means we cannot just ignore the manifestations, because it would make us unable to comprehend the whole as well as its core, which is *Tao*.

So, we need to be both free from and full of desire.

Although the quote examined here is not to be found in *Tao Te Ching*, I find it plausible that it is an interpretation of the lines about desire in the first chapter. It doesn't encompass all that Lao Tzu intended with the chapter, but it's a good start.

The oldest book I have found to contain the quote is

from as late as 2014: *Lao Zi: His Words*, by Daniel Coenn. It is an ebook containing 225 quotes and aphorisms supposed to be from Lao Tzu, probably collected on the Internet. There are no sources given, just the quotes.

The other four books with the quote are all from 2016 and accrediting Lao Tzu.

On the web, the earliest occurrence of the quote with an ascertained date is in a blog post from May 2010, also ascribing it to Lao Tzu. The first posting of the quote on Facebook was in July 2012. But it must have been up on Goodreads before that, since the quote got its first like there already on February 1, 2008. That might be where this quote got started.

I have not found any initial source to the quote or reference to a specific *Tao Te Ching* version and chapter. It seems to be inspired by the first chapter and then paraphrased, to say the least, but I could not confirm that.

Violence, even well intentioned

"Violence, even well intentioned, always rebounds upon oneself."

Lao Tzu did not speak of violence as such, but he was clear about his dislike of armed forces and war, and pointed it out more than once in *Tao Te Ching*. Chapter 31 starts (my version):

> *Weapons are ominous tools.*
> *They are abhorred by all creatures.*
> *Anyone who follows the Way shuns them.*

In chapter 30 Lao Tzu described his reason for condemning war further. Simply put, the price is too high for both the loser and the winner:

> *Those who advice the ruler on the Way,*
> *Do not want the world subdued with weapons.*
> *Such deeds bring on retaliation.*
> *Thorn bushes grow where armies have camped.*
> *Battles are followed by years of famine.*

This is actually the chapter from which the quote discussed here is taken, but in the widely popular *Tao Te Ching* version by Stephen Mitchell from 1988. His rendering of the above part, ending with the quote, reads:

> *Whoever relies on the Tao in governing men*
> *doesn't try to force issues*
> *or defeat enemies by force of arms.*
> *For every force there is a counterforce.*
> *Violence, even well intentioned,*
> *always rebounds upon oneself.*

His whole interpretation of this part of chapter 30 is confusing. He focused on the mutual losses in battle, but Lao Tzu worried more about what it did to the land and the people. His interpretation is not shared by other versions. To give another example, here is James Legge's from 1891 (page 72):

> *He who would assist a lord of men in harmony with the Tâo will not assert his mastery in the kingdom by force of arms. Such a course is sure to meet with its proper return.*
>
> *Wherever a host is stationed, briars and thorns spring up. In the sequence of great armies there are sure to be bad years.*

Mitchell missed the powerful imagery of the thorns and the dire consequence of bad years and famine, and in particular he neglected the suffering of all those who were not soldiers in the war. In every war, they tend to be the majority.

For more about Stephen Mitchell and his version of *Tao Te Ching*, see the chapter "A good traveler has no fixed plans."

Watch your thoughts

"Watch your thoughts, they become your words; watch your words, they become your actions; watch your actions, they become your habits; watch your habits, they become your character; watch your character, it becomes your destiny."

This long quote, often accredited to Lao Tzu, has a simplistic and repetitious style that is similar to his writing, and at least the first two lines would fit within *Tao Te Ching* – but the concepts of habits, character, and destiny much less so.

Lao Tzu certainly described human behavior that could be categorized as habits, but he would not explain them that way. According to him, people do what they do mainly out of ignorance. Character is also something distant from Lao Tzu's view that people are really the same, they just act differently. It's not a question of personality, but again of ignorance versus wisdom. It's not about how people are, but what they do or don't do.

And destiny is a far too deterministic expression of the simple fact that actions have consequences. To Lao Tzu, everything would be possible to correct, usually by avoiding action. Then problems would be solved by themselves, because that is how nature works.

There are examples of the type of chain of consequences described in this quote, also in *Tao Te Ching*. None with the same or similar content, though. One such instance is in chapter 38 (my version):

When the Way is lost there is virtue.
When virtue is lost there is benevolence.
When benevolence is lost there is righteousness.
When righteousness is lost there are rituals.
Rituals are the end of fidelity and honesty,
And the beginning of confusion.

The quote examined here is definitely not from *Tao Te Ching*, not even from any distorted version of it that I have come across. But Lao Tzu is far from the only one to whom the quote has been accredited. Among the others are Mahatma Gandhi, Margaret Thatcher, Charles Reade, and the Buddha.

Garson O'Toole has thoroughly tracked down the history of this quote on his website Quote Investigator (quoteinvestigator.com/2013/01/10/watch-your-thoughts/).

A very similar wording was accredited to Bishop Beckwaith (probably a misspelling of John W. Beckwith, 1831-1890) in a newspaper from 1885:

Plant a thought and reap a word;
plant a word and reap an action;
plant an action and reap a habit;
plant a habit and reap a character;
plant a character and reap a destiny.

Both before and after that occurrence, versions with more or less different wordings have been published. An almost identical wording of the quote discussed here was published in a Texas newspaper in 1977, accrediting it to Frank Outlaw, who had been the President of the Bi-Lo chain of stores:

Watch your thoughts, they become words;
watch your words, they become actions;
watch your actions, they become habits;
watch your habits, they become character;
watch your character, for it becomes your destiny.

During the following years, several other newspapers printed the quote, also naming Frank Outlaw as its origin. Soon, it appeared in books, too. The earliest one I found is from 1983: *A Treasury of Days*, by Dee Danner Barwick (page 23).

As for accrediting the quote to Lao Tzu, the earliest example Garson O'Toole found is from the website Goodreads in2010, the date deducted by the first comment on the quote there being from January 2, 2010. That link seems to fail now (August 2020), probably due to Goodreads site changes. The present web page with the quote only has likes since March, 2017.

On Facebook I found the first post of the quote already from November 17, 2005, giving no source to it. The first Facebook quote accrediting it to Lao Tzu was October 14, 2009.

In printed books, I found the earliest crediting to Lao Tzu of this quote in *My life with the green & gold* from 2013, by the sportscaster Jessie Garcia (page 186).

What the caterpillar calls the end

"What the caterpillar calls the end, the rest of the world calls a butterfly."

This is an amusing saying, but it has one flaw: what is the point of view of the butterfly? It would make more sense if the perspective of the caterpillar was countered with that of the butterfly. The rest of the world would probably not care as much. What the caterpillar regards as the end, the butterfly must see as the beginning.

Anyway, though often accredited with this quote, Lao Tzu mentioned neither caterpillars nor butterflies in *Tao Te Ching*. He might have appreciated the humor of it, but it is not the kind of joke he would make. There is another legendary Taoist much more likely to have said something of this kind. That is Chuang Tzu, who lived in the 4th century BC.

The most famous anecdote in the texts about him concerns a butterfly. Here it is in James Legge's *Texts of Taoism*, volume 1, from 1891 (page 197):

Formerly, I, Kwang Kau, dreamt that I was a butterfly, a butterfly flying about, feeling that it was enjoying itself. I did not know that it was Kau. Suddenly I awoke, and was myself again, the veritable Kau. I did not know whether it had formerly been Kau dreaming that he was a butterfly, or it was now a butterfly dreaming that it was Kau. But between Kau and a butterfly there must be a difference. This is a case of what is called the Transformation of Things.

This anecdote, from the end of book 2 in *Chuang Tzu*, is probably the reason for a different wording of the quote examined here often on the web being falsely attributed to Chuang Tzu:

Just when the caterpillar thought the world was over, it became a butterfly.

There is another wording, which is even closer to the quote discussed here:

What the caterpillar calls the end of the world, the master calls a butterfly.

This one is from the 1977 book *Illusions*, by Richard Bach (page 177). In his novel, he presented this and other maxims sprayed across the book as coming from *Messiah's Handbook*, which is as fictional as the rest of the novel – as far as I know. The quote is at the start of the last chapter of the book, with this line preceding it:

The mark of your ignorance is the depth of your belief in injustice and tragedy.

Since I have not found any source to the quote examined here older than Bach's book, I must assume that it is a slightly altered version of his maxim. As far as I know, the quote's earliest appearance with the exact wording (not Bach's) is in a Dutch book from the year 2000: *Scenario's voor kennisomgevingen* (*Scenarios for Knowledge Environments*), by Foks, Hofman, and Kokhuis (page 75). They accredited the quote to Lao Tzu, as has every book since – when naming a source.

I doubt that this book got a huge score of readers, especially since it is in the Dutch language, except for the quote. But in 2008, three books with the quote were published, all ascribing it to Lao Tzu: *With the Dawn Rejoicing*, by Melannie Svoboda (page 80), *Mastering the Light*, by George Lewis (page 43), and the Hallmark book *1001 Things to Be Thankful For* (#934 of the things listed). My guess is that the last one was spread the most.

A Google search finds the oldest posting of the exact quote from March 2005, giving no source to it, and the next from August 2008 in a blog, ascribing the quote to Lao Tzu. On Facebook, the earliest appearance of the quote is from May 2010, also ascribing it to Lao Tzu. That accreditation has since been repeated when the quote was.

On Goodreads, both Richard Bach's version of the quote and that ascribed to Lao Tzu are listed. The former has likes back to 2008 and the latter back to April 11, 2010.

When I let go of what I am

"When I let go of what I am, I become what I might be."

This quote is weird not only in the eyes of Lao Tzu, but in those of just about every ancient thinker. They would all agree that I have to be what I am – that's the path worth taking. What I might be is just an illusion, making the mind fool itself.

It makes sense in our modern zeitgeist, where everyone from a young age wants to be famous and spectacular. Like in the American credo: you can be anything you want to be. Good luck with that.

Lao Tzu, in particular, would sneer at such ambitions. Modesty was his ideal. Returning to the natural way was his recipe. Not chasing some gilded dream that would disappoint even more if it were reached.

The trick, every sage of the past would tell you, is to be who you are. In short: this quote is plain nonsense.

On some websites, there is another sentence added to the quote:

When I let go of what I have, I receive what I need.

That has an anti-materialistic ring to it, which Lao Tzu and Jesus alike would appreciate. But they might prefer to reverse it to something like: you should not have what you don't need.

Both quotes are from a wildly tendentious version of

Tao Te Ching by John Heider: *The Tao of Leadership* from 1985. It seems to have no intention of being true to the original.

The two quotes (page 43) are very loosely based on the first lines of chapter 22 of *Tao Te Ching* — so loosely that it is hard to comprehend how Heider got to this interpretation.

Here is my version of the start of chapter 22:

Hulk to be whole.
Bend to be straight.
Empty to be filled.
Wear down to be renewed.
Reduce to gain.
Excess confuses.

And here is D. C. Lau's from 1963 (page 79):

Bowed down then preserved;
Bent then straight;
Hollow then full;
Worn then new;
A little then benefited;
A lot then perplexed.

So, it's not about changing one's personality, but one's actions.

For more about John Heider and his *Tao Te Ching* version, see the chapter "Silence is a source."

When pure sincerity forms

"When pure sincerity forms within, it is outwardly realized in other people's hearts."

This statement, accredited to Lao Tzu, is strange. Where could sincerity form other than within (a person's mind), and how can people's hearts be something outward? If the sentence would be trimmed and simplified it might make more sense, for example: one person's sincerity can be recognized by others. And that's no sensational revelation.

Lao Tzu did state in many ways that the wisdom and insight of the sage would convince people, if not expressed in a pompous fashion. Spoken with humility, the truth will be accepted. Already in chapter 2 of *Tao Te Ching* it is stated about the sage (my version):

Because he demands no honor,
He will never be dishonored.

And in chapter 49:

People turn their eyes and ears to him,
And the sage cares for them like his own children.

Also, in chapter 66:

Because he does not resist,
None in the world resists him.

The source to the quote discussed here is not *Tao Te Ching*, but a later Taoist text called *Wen Tzu* after its presumed writer. According to the tradition, Wen Tzu was a direct student of Lao Tzu, contemporary to Confucius (551-479 BC). That was not necessarily the case.

The oldest version of the text is from the tomb of a person who died in 55 BC, but may originally have been composed around 200 BC. It was discovered in 1973, reported in 1981, and the transcription of it in Chinese was published in 1995. The previously established version of the text is likely to have been composed at least 400 years later, not earlier than the 3rd century CE.

The two versions differ mainly in that the newer one has Lao Tzu answer questions from Wen Tzu, whereas the older one has Wen Tzu as the teacher answering questions from a student of his.

The English translation of Wen Tzu containing the exact quote discussed here is *Further Teachings of Lao-tzu* from 1991 by Thomas Cleary (page 20). As already the title indicates, it is based on the later version of the Wen Tzu text. Thus, the quote is accredited to Lao Tzu instead of Wen Tzu.

There is not yet a complete English translation of the older text, but Paul van Els has written extensively about it in his doctoral thesis from 2006 and in a book published 2018.

Considering the finding of the older version of the Wen Tzu text, it is safe to say that the quote should not be accredited to Lao Tzu.

When the student is ready

"When the student is ready the teacher will appear. When the student is truly ready the teacher will disappear."

This is a complex one. To cut the story short, this is not a Lao Tzu quote. The only thing he had to say about students is in chapter 41 (my version):

The superior student listens to the Way
And follows it closely.
The average student listens to the Way
And follows some and some not.
The lesser student listens to the Way
And laughs out loud.
If there were no laughter it would not be the Way.

There is no certainty that he had any students at all, at least not in a formal way. If he did, he probably would not regard their meeting as some mechanism of destiny. Furthermore, as chapter 41 indicates, the student's only real teacher is *Tao*, the Way – and that never disappears, since it is the very fabric of the world, as Lao Tzu saw it. No mere human can replace that teacher, so we can only hope to be its students and learn.

That said, it is interesting to cut the saying in half to trace its background. The first part, "When the student is ready the teacher will appear," has a long history, being accredited to Buddhism, Zen Buddhism in particular, European occultism, and so on.

In 2013, this saying and its history was treated extensively on the blog Fake Buddha Quotes (fakebuddhaquotes.com) by Bodhipaksa (his Buddhist name). His conclusion was that the quote stemmed from the 1885 book *Light on the Path*, by Mabel Collins (1851-1927), though with a slightly different wording:

For when the disciple is ready the Master is ready also.

As Bodhipaksa points out in his text, there are alternative wordings of the saying. The student is sometimes called pupil, disciple, or seeker, and the teacher is sometimes called master. That is hardly significant. But there is indeed a difference between "is ready also" and "will appear." The latter suggests that fate is involved, a mystical link between student and teacher bringing them together. The version written by Mabel Collins merely says that when the student is ready the teacher is, too, like when a class starts at school.

Bodhipaksa found versions of the saying in texts of Theosophy, the movement founded by Madame Blavatsky and others in 1875. A Theosophical publication, *The Herald of the Star*, had this version in 1914:

When the pupil is ready, the Master will appear.

Similar versions appeared within Theosophy the following years. Still I wonder if this quote is of Theosophical invention. It has an ancient ring to it that suggests previous spiritual sources, in Europe or elsewhere. Unfortunately, I have not been able to find them.

To my knowledge, the earliest book with the wording "the teacher appears" is *Fourteen Lessons in Yogi Philosophy and Oriental Occultism* from 1905, by Yogi Ramacharaka, pseudonym for William Walker Atkinson (1862-1932). He wrote (page 270f):

> *Remember this — it is a great occult truth — when the student is ready the teacher appears — the way will be opened to you step by step, and as each new spiritual need comes into existence, the means to satisfy it will be on the way.*

Atkinson was also involved in the publishing of *The Kybalion: a Study of the Hermetic Philosophy of Ancient Egypt and Greece* from 1908, written by "Three Initiates" whereof he was surely one or maybe all. It is supposed to transmit the teaching of the legendary figure Hermes Trismegistus, a favorite among occultists for many centuries. It contains a saying close to what is discussed here (pages 12 and 23):

> *When the ears of the student are ready to hear, then cometh the lips to fill them with wisdom.*

The book of poems and quotes *Continuation II* from 1990, by Louis Dudek (1918-2001), accredits Hermes Trismegistus with the quote "When the student is ready the teacher appears" (page 103), which may be a mix-up between the quote from *The Kybalion* and some other source. *Dawn of the New Day* from 1947, by Vitvan, gives the same quote followed by a comment on Hermes Trismegistus, which may have given the impression of the quote being from him (page 12). There are several web pages that seem to have made the same mistake.

The second part of the quote examined here, with the teacher disappearing, makes no sense without the first part. But the whole saying has a flare of Zen to it. The paradox of the teacher appearing when needed, and disappearing when the student is truly ready to be taught, has sort of a *koan* quality, a riddle that brings a great realization when solved. It means that students who have progressed enough can be their own teachers. Still, the quote has mainly been accredited to Lao Tzu.

The idea of the student becoming complete, and thereby ceasing to be a student, is expressed in *Confucian Analects*, Book XIX, where disciples of Confucius are speaking (James Legge, *The Chinese Classics*, volume 1, 1893, page 344):

> Tsze-hsiâ said, 'The officer, having discharged all his duties, should devote his leisure to learning. The student, having completed his learning, should apply himself to be an officer.'

There is a saying taking the concept even farther, suggesting that there might be no need for a teacher at all, if the student is apt:

> A diligent student needs no teacher.

It is often accredited to Confucius or his disciples, since it was discussed in the ancient texts what teacher he himself might have had—or if he at all ever needed one. On the website Quora, the signature Lycke Li goes through several Confucian texts where the subject has been discussed, though nowhere exactly with the wording of the saying.

As for the student and teacher quote examined here, the earliest example of the complete quote on the web with an asserted date is on Goodreads, where it got its first like on August 27, 2014. It is ascribed to Lao Tzu. The earliest books with the whole quote are from 2016, also ascribing it to Lao Tzu, without giving a source.

On Facebook, the earliest example of the first half of the quote is from July 21, 2007, calling it a Buddhist proverb. The following years, a number of Facebook posts of the half quote ascribed it to Buddha. The earliest Facebook post I have found with the complete quote examined here is from December 9, 2015, accrediting it to Lao Tzu. It wrote "appears" instead for "will appear," and so did several persons repeating the quote.

I have no idea how the quote got ascribed to Lao Tzu, or for that matter how it appeared at all. Its second half is a clever comment on the first part, so it is likely to stem from the same tradition, which is Theosophy and other occult teachings, from the late 19th and early 20th centuries – maybe under some influence from speculations about Zen, which grew in the Western world during the 20th century.

There is a more recent source to the second half quote, which might be its origin: *Shadows of the sacred: Seeing through Spiritual Illusions* from 1995, by the transpersonal psychologist Frances E. Vaughan (1935-2017). Discussing the necessity of reaching independence of a teacher, she wrote (page 248):

Leaving a teacher can be just as important as finding a teacher at the appropriate time. We might say that when the student is ready, the teacher disappears.

Earlier in the book, discussing how a spiritual teacher is found, she wrote (page 188):

When the student is ready, a teacher appears.

In both cases she did not mark these words as quotes. She may have come up with them herself, or regarded these kinds of thoughts so generic it was not necessary to point out a source. Still, as far as I have found, her book is the first one with the part about the teacher disappearing.

When you are content

"When you are content to be simply yourself and don't compare or compete, everyone will respect you."

So much in this sentence deviates from the perspectives of Lao Tzu. Comparing and competing is an obsession of modern man, but hardly of the people of ancient China. The idea of being oneself, too, is quite anachronistic. Lao Tzu would ask: What else can one be? Also "everyone will respect you" fits our days better than those of Lao Tzu.

But behind this modern lingo, thoughts similar to those of Lao Tzu can be detected. To be content without strife and allow one's life to be simple is what Lao Tzu recommended. The one who lives so will gain the admiration of others.

Lo and behold, this quote is found in a popular version of *Tao Te Ching* from 1988, written by Stephen Mitchell. His version has been the most bestselling one for years, and still is. He allowed himself plenty of poetic license to make Lao Tzu's text accessible to modern man.

The quote is from the end of chapter 8. His version of the chapter is decently close to the original text at times, but at others it deviates considerably. That's particularly evident in the last lines. The words and meaning of the lines are there, but Mitchell's addition about being yourself sticks out. That turns the perspective away from Lao Tzu's idea.

For comparison, here is my version of the end of chapter 8:

Where there is no conflict, there is no fault.

Where I wrote "conflict" it is also possible to write competition, or for that matter strife or struggle. D. C. Lau used "contend" in his 1963 version, where he had the whole chapter be about the good example of water (page 64):

It is because it does not contend that it is never at fault.

Furthermore, my wording "no fault" can be interpreted as in the eyes of others, which is indeed an expression of respect. That is how James Legge understood it in 1891 (page 53):

And when (one with the highest excellence) does not wrangle (about his low position), no one finds fault with him.

So, the remaining problem with Mitchell's version is that thing about being yourself. It is superfluous and leads the reader astray. Lao Tzu was not much for self-reflection. As so often in *Tao Te Ching*, what the end of chapter 8 points out is not to overdo things. Bernhard Karlgren in 1975 simply translated it (page 2):

If one does not strive there will be no blame.

For more about Stephen Mitchell and his version of *Tao Te Ching*, see the chapter "A good traveler has no fixed plans."

When you find the way

"When you find the way
others will find you.
Passing by on the road
they will be drawn to your door.
The way that cannot be heard
will be echoed in your voice.
The way that cannot be seen
will be reflected in your eyes."

These are not the words of Lao Tzu, but the quote partly reflects what *Tao Te Ching* states about following *Tao*, the Way. Chapter 35 reads (my version):

> *Hold on to the great image,*
> *And the whole world follows,*
> *Follows unharmed,*
> *Content and completely at peace.*
>
> *Music and food make the traveler halt.*
> *But words spoken about the Way have no taste.*
> *When looked at, there's not enough to see.*
> *When listened to, there's not enough to hear.*
> *When used, it is never exhausted.*

The similarities between the quote examined here and this chapter of *Tao Te Ching* makes me suspect that it is a rather free interpretation of that chapter's message. Its gravest anomaly is the focus on the person instead of the principle. It is all about you and yours, whereas Lao Tzu insisted that the sage would be almost invisible because of modesty. Chapter 77 states:

> *The sage acts without taking credit.*
> *He accomplishes without dwelling on it.*
> *He does not want to display his worth.*

Still, the source to the quote discussed here claims it to be from *Tao Te Ching*. It appeared in *Real Magic: Creating Miracles in Everyday Life*, by Wayne W. Dyer, published in 1992 (page 106).

He said nothing about what version of the Lao Tzu text he got it from, and I have not found it – not even in his own version of *Tao Te Ching* from 2008. He must have allowed himself some extensive poetic license in this version, and it is most likely based on chapter 35.

Dyer's version of that chapter in *Living the Wisdom of the Tao* from 2008 (page 73) has no likeness to the quote examined here, nor is it more faithful to standard translations of the text. Some of the lines are influenced, to say the least, by Jonathan Star's 2001 version of the chapter (page 48) and the last three lines follow almost completely Stephen Mitchell's 1988 version (page 35).

It is strange that Dyer would more or less improvise the long quote examined here and claim it to be from Lao Tzu. In his 1992 book, Dyer quoted Lao Tzu three times more, neglecting to mention his sources. But they are easy enough to find. On page 72 he quoted the last lines of Arthur Waley's 1934 version of chapter 11 in *Tao Te Ching* (page 155), with the only change of replacing one word with a synonym. On page 126 he quoted a part of chapter 25 from *Tao: The Watercourse Way*, 1975, by Alan Watts (page 41). On page 230 he used the same source for part of chapter 38 (page 109).

Just the quote examined here remains a mystery. Its source is found if "the way" is replaced by "the TAO," which is what Benjamin Hoff wrote in his version of *Tao Te Ching* from 1981, called *The Way to Life: At the Heart of the Tao Te Ching*. Hoff is most famous for the book he published the following year – *The Tao of Pooh*, where he had Winnie the Pooh explain Taoism.

The quote examined here is the beginning of Hoff's version of chapter 35. Dyer only made the little change to "the way." Hoff's wording deviates much more than that from the standard translations. My version is given above. Here is how chapter 35 begins in Philip J. Ivanhoe's version from 2002 (page 35):

Hold on to the great image and the whole world will come to you.
They will come and suffer no harm;
They will be peaceful, secure, and prosperous.

The great image is Tao, of course. As for the rest of Hoff's version, he must have gotten carried away by some poetic urge, adding a bundle of words and making the whole thing seem like idolatry.

Another quote from Hoff's *Tao Te Ching* version is discussed in the chapter "Stop leaving." For more about Wayne W. Dyer and his interpretations, see the chapter "Every human being's essential nature."

Why do you run around

"Why do you run around looking for the truth? Be still, and there it is – in the mountain, in the pine, in yourself."

I would imagine that Lao Tzu was not much for running, for whatever reason. He would surely also agree that if you can't find the truth while being still, you are not likely to find it running around.

The truth was to Lao Tzu nothing but *Tao*, the Way. In my version of *Tao Te Ching* the word "truth" does not appear even once, nor does it in several other versions I checked. James Legge in 1891 used it twice – in chapter 21 and 41, both referring to *Tao* being that truth.

But certainly, *Tao* can be found anywhere – in the mountain, the pine, and oneself, as well as everywhere else. To Lao Tzu, *Tao* was the source and ruler of everything in the world.

Still, the quote examined here is not from Lao Tzu. But he stated something similar in chapter 47 of *Tao Te Ching* (my version):

Without stepping out the door,
You can know the world.
Without looking through the window,
You can see Heaven's Way.
The longer you travel, the less you know.
Therefore:
The sage knows without traveling,

Perceives without looking,
Completes without acting.

I have not found the exact quote discussed here in any book search, and on the Internet it seems not to have appeared until a few years ago. I did not even find it on the Goodreads website.

It may have started in 2016 with a meme produced by the website Chill-app, with an image of cloudy mountains and the quote accredited to Lao Tzu. Its first appearance on Facebook, as far as I have found, was in a post dated 22 October 2016.

It is possible that the quote is a poetic license paraphrasing of chapter 47 in *Tao Te Ching*, but I have not been able to confirm that. It seems to be so recent that I rather suspect it to be a contemporary effort at ancient wisdom, based on nothing in particular.

Your own positive future

"Your own positive future begins in this moment. All you have is right now. Every goal is possible from here."

Whether positive of negative, where else could your future begin but at this moment? That is the very definition of the future, just as the definition of the past is what happened before the present moment.

The second sentence is equally self-evident, since we can say nothing for certain about the future, and the past is already gone. But it also tells us that at any moment we can redirect our lives, at least to the extent circumstances permit – which leads to the third sentence.

I am not sure that every goal is possible, but most of them are at least possible to strive for. In other words – few goals are definitely impossible, as long as we stay within the borders of what natural law permits and a human being can muster.

This is not a Lao Tzu quote, although often referred to as such on the Internet, but there is a very famous saying of his from which it can be concluded. In chapter 64 of *Tao Te Ching* it is stated (my version):

> *A climb of eight hundred feet*
> *Starts where the foot stands.*

D. C. Lau in 1963 used a wording that is much more recognizable and common (page 125):

A journey of a thousand miles
Starts from beneath one's feet.

I made my different choice based primarily on the support of both Mawangdui manuscripts from around 200 BC, which leave no doubt. My source was Robert G. Henricks in 1989 (page 150). Still, the essence of the message is the same.

What Lao Tzu was really pointing out was not the vast scope of opportunity at each moment, but the fact that things are so much easier to deal with at the outset and when going carefully step by step. It is not an equivalent of the popular American expression that you can be anything you want to be. Instead it speaks, as Lao Tzu often did, about being perceptive and careful. The first part of the chapter makes it clear:

Stillness is easy to maintain.
What has not yet emerged is easy to prevent.
The brittle is easy to shatter.
The small is easy to scatter.
Solve it before it happens.
Order it before chaos emerges.

A tree as wide as a man's embrace
Grows from a tiny shoot.
A tower of nine stories
Starts with a pile of dirt.
A climb of eight hundred feet
Starts where the foot stands.

Later in this unusually long chapter of *Tao Te Ching*, there is a warning again stressing the need to be careful throughout:

People fail at the threshold of success.
Be as cautious at the end as at the beginning.

In spite of the differences of perspective in the quote examined here and the words of chapter 64, it is plausible that the former is some paraphrasing extraction of the latter. Maybe it is an expansion of the idea in the line about how any voyage begins where you stand.

One example of linking chapter 64 to the message of the quote discussed here is in *Change Your Thoughts, Change Your Life* from 2007, by Wayne W. Dyer (page 303):

The essence of the widely known 64th verse of the Tao Te Ching is this: Every goal is possible from here!

Still, Dyer's wording of chapter 64 in his own version of *Tao Te Ching* from 2008, *Living the Wisdom of the Tao*, does not contain the quote, but follows the standard rather closely, also for the line discussed here (page 131):

A journey of a thousand miles begins with a single step.

There is nothing unique in the message of the quote. The idea that one can create one's own future at any moment is a popular one, especially in self-realization circles. Here is an example from 1989, in *Spiritual Growth: Being Your Higher Self*, by Sanaya Roman (page 124):

You can create your own positive future and you can choose any reality you want.

The oldest book I have found with the exact quote is *Yoga Mama, Yoga Baby* from 2013, by Margo Shapiro Bachman, accrediting it to Lao Tzu (page 236). There is no mention of a source, but I would be surprised if the quote was not taken from the Internet.

The earliest ascertained Internet occurrence of the quote I have found is on the Goodreads site, where it is ascribed to Lao Tzu and got its first like on June 28, 2009. On Facebook the first occurrence of the quote seems to have been on July 5, 2012, with a post that was soon shared 18 times and reached 54 likes. The quote was written in both English and Spanish, and accredited to Lao Tzu.

I have not been able to find where this quote originated, or if it did so already from the start ascribing it to Lao Tzu. My best guess is still that it somehow was extracted and distorted from chapter 64 of *Tao Te Ching* – or from Dyer's interpretation of it, mentioned above.

For more on Wayne W. Dyer and his Lao Tzu quotes, see the chapter "Every human being's essential nature."

Literature

There's a forest of books about Taoism, Lao Tzu, and *Tao Te Ching*. It makes no sense to list them all, so I have chosen a few English versions of *Tao Te Ching* that I value or find significant in the continued exploration of Lao Tzu's thoughts. Less important works are also included if they have made an imprint in other literature or on the Internet.

The subject is popular, so new books will appear as you read this, but I believe that some of the sources listed below will not that quickly be obsolete. Others, though, might be found less adequate and fade away.

The books are listed alphabetically after the names of the persons writing the versions. I have added a short comment to every version listed, mainly regarding its content and style of translation.

Notice that the list below does not contain every version of *Tao Te Ching* discussed in this book. Those excluded here are sufficiently presented in the chapters where they are mentioned. That also goes for other books discussed, as well as Internet sources.

As for the Taoism resources on the Internet, they change so quickly that I can only recommend a Google search (or whatever search engine is the most prominent one, when you read this). Notice that different spellings give partly different search results. For example, Tao Te Ching, Dao De Jing, and Daodejing searches may differ, although the major search engines now regard them as synonymous. The same is true for Lao Tzu, Lao Zi, and Laozi. Many complete translations of *Tao Te Ching* are available on the web.

Tao Te Ching Versions

Ames, Roger T. & Hall, David L.: DAO DE JING
New York, Ballantine 2003.
A knowledgeable and rather daring version, focusing on philosophical aspects, which also presents the text in Chinese. The 1993 findings in Guodian are richly presented and included in the interpretation.

Balfour, Frederic Henry: TAOIST TEXTS
London, Trubner & Co., 1884
This old version includes the Chinese text of *Tao Te Ching* and a translation that tends to be a bit over-explanatory, maybe also outdated, reminding of James Legge's version. The comments are knowledgeable.

Blakney, Raymond B.: THE WAY OF LIFE
USA, New American Library 1955.
A straightforward and clear version of the text, but it often seems like paraphrasing, although he added what he called a "Paraphrase" version to each chapter. Neither version is near the standard translations.

Bynner, Witter: THE WAY OF LIFE ACCORDING TO LAOTZU
New York, Day 1944.
An American version, which is also its subtitle. It is based on English versions of that time. In the effort to clarify the

chapters, Bynner allowed himself to deviate quite far from Lao Tzu's text.

Carus, Paul: LAO-TZE'S TAO-TEH-KING
Chicago, Open Court Publishing 1898.
This knowledgeable text presents Taoism and Lao Tzu, with a word by word translation of *Tao Te Ching* including the Chinese text, and his own version where *Tao* is translated as "Reason." That choice is possible, but rare.

Chalmers, John: THE SPECULATIONS ON METAPHYSICS, POLITY, AND MORALITY OF "THE OLD PHILOSOPHER," LAU-TSZE
London, Trübner 1868.
This is the first translation into English of *Tao Te Ching*. The text is occasionally elaborate from striving to be true to the original, but by that it is also quite trustworthy.

Chan, Wing-tsit: THE WAY OF LAO TZU
Indianapolis, Bobbs-Merrrril 1963.
The professor of Chinese culture and philosophy wrote a learned and trustworthy version, with each chapter richly commented. The book also contains bibliographies in Western and Eastern languages on the subject.

Chen, Ellen M.: THE TAO TE CHING
New York, Paragon 1989.
With a knowledge that is only surpassed by the categorical attitude, Chen's version includes but is far from dominated by the Mawangdui manuscripts. Lots of facts are added, as well as far-reaching personal interpretations of Taoist philosophy and how to apply it.

Cheng, Man-jan: LAO TZU: MY WORDS ARE VERY EASY TO UNDERSTAND
California, North Atlantic Books 1981. Translated by Tam C. Gibbs.
Cheng has commented the chapters of the text in short lessons, focused on the principles of Taoism. The explanations are so short that they don't add much to the text itself. The Chinese text is included in the book.

Cleary, Thomas: THE ESSENTIAL TAO
San Francisco, Harper Collins 1993.
Cleary has translated several Taoist and Buddhist texts, which have been published in a number of different volumes. This one contains the texts of both Lao Tzu and Chuang Tzu. His translation is competent, although his choice of words is sometimes odd, deviating from the usual solutions.

Crowley, Aleister: THE TAO TEH KING
1918. Several editions in print.
The famous occultist made his own very personal interpretation of the text, where the hexagrams of I Ching have also been used. Crowley is always worth reading, although it's not certain that he speaks according to the *Tao* of Lao Tzu.

Duyvendak, J. J. L.: TAO TE CHING
London, Murray 1954.
This professor of Chinese filled his version of the text with elaborate comments, including linguistic and philosophical aspects. Unfortunately, it is since long out of print.

Feng, Gia-fu & English, Jane: LAO TSU: TAO TE CHING
London, Wildwood 1972.
This version is simple and rewarding, although it isn't al-

ways in accordance with prevalent opinion. It lacks commentaries, but is richly illustrated with both calligraphy of the chapters and mood-filled photographs. This book has since its release contributed greatly to the popularization of *Tao Te Ching*. A revised edition was published in 1989.

Giles, Lionel: THE SAYINGS OF LAO TZU
London, Orient Press 1904.
In this translation the chapters have been completely re-ordered according to themes, not even stating what established chapters they belong to, which makes the book very hard to use as a reference. But both Lionel and his father Herbert Giles were esteemed sinologists, translating several Chinese classics.

Henricks, Robert G.: TE-TAO CHING
New York, Ballantine 1989.
The professor of religion manages a very trustworthy version of the text, based primarily on the manuscripts of Mawangdui. Because of their order of the chapters, he has reversed the words of the title. His comments are knowledgeable and precise. The Mawangdui texts in Chinese are also included. This is a major work on the Mawangdui findings.

Henricks, Robert G.: LAO TZU'S TAO TE CHING
New York, Columbia University Press 2000.
In this book, Henricks concentrates on the findings in Guodian, which are competently presented and examined. They are also compared to the Mawangdui and Wang Pi versions. The texts are included in Chinese. The problem with the book is that the order of the chapters is according to the findings, which makes it difficult to use as a reference.

Hoff, Benjamin: THE WAY TO LIFE: AT THE HEART OF THE TAO TE CHING
Weatherhill 1981.
This version makes some odd wording choices that are far from standard translations. The year after this book was published Hoff released *The Tao of Pooh*, which became an international bestseller and contributed to making Lao Tzu something of a household name.

Ivanhoe, Philip J.: THE DAODEJING OF LAOZI
New York, Seven Bridges Press 2002.
The historian of Chinese thought has made a straightforward and clean translation of the text, a learned introduction to it, and comparisons between other translations. There are also many informative notes.

Julien, Stanislas: LE LIVRE DE LA VOIE ET DE LA VERTU
Paris 1842.
Julien was a professor in Chinese at the Paris University. His French version is the first printed one in a Western language. It is still in print, as a facsimile. Unfortunately, there is no English translation of it.

Karlgren, Bernhard: NOTES ON LAO-TSE
Bulletin of Östasiatiska Museet, nr. 47/1975. Offprint.
The prominent Swedish sinologist finally published, just three years before his demise, a version of the text. He did so in a way as modest as was his habit – in a magazine of the Stockholm East Asian Museum. His interpretation is precise and clarifying, but the comments are minimal. At the time of his interpretation, the findings in Mawangdui were not at his disposal.

Karlgren, Bernhard: THE POETICAL PARTS OF LAO-TSI
Göteborgs Högskolas årsskrift 1932:3
This essay goes through all the rhymes of *Tao Te Ching* in ancient or archaic Chinese.

Lau, D.C.: LAO TZU: TAO TE CHING
London, Penguin 1963.
This professor of Chinese literature gave a knowledgeable and clear interpretation of the text. The book also contains explicit comments and explanations. In later editions of this book, Lau included the findings in Mawangdui and Guodian.

Legge, James: THE TEXTS OF TAOISM volume 1 & 2
London, Oxford 1891.
The first volume contains *Tao Te Ching* and books I-XVII of Chuang Tzu, and the second volume Chuang Tzu XVIII-XXXIII and some other Taoist texts. Legge's historically significant version has extensive explanations with many references to the Chinese pictograms and their meaning. Still, his translation is aged, especially because of its effort to create poetry, which sometimes makes it deviate considerably from the wording of the original.

Le Guin, Ursula K. & Seaton, J. P.: LAO TZU: TAO TE CHING
Boston, Shambhala 1997.
The famous fantasy and science fiction writer made an elegant and very clear version of the text, in collaboration with a professor of Chinese. There are some comments, especially on how the chapters should be understood and on linguistic aspects.

Mair, Victor H.: TAO TE CHING
New York, Bantam 1990.
This professor of Chinese based his competent and clear translation on the Mawangdui manuscripts. The book also contains extensive comments, especially those comparing the text somewhat surprisingly with the ideas of ancient India.

Maurer, Herrymon: TAO: THE WAY OF THE WAYS
England, Wildwood 1986.
These interpretations and comments are aimed at explaining the text's spiritual content, which is done quite cryptically at times. In spite of the late date of this version, Maurer was unfamiliar with the Mawangdui manuscripts.

Miles, Thomas H.: TAO TE CHING: ABOUT THE WAY OF NATURE AND ITS POWERS
New York, Avery Publishing 1992.
This professor of English has made a gentle and straightforward version, faithful to the original. The book also contains, among other things, explanatory texts on fundamental concepts of Taoism and ancient Chinese thought.

Mitchell, Stephen: TAO TE CHING: A NEW ENGLISH VERSION
USA, Harper & Row 1988.
This very popular version, with limited comments, seems to lack noticeable knowledge of the Mawangdui manuscripts. It has its merits as a simple and direct interpretation of the text, though frequently getting very far from the standard translations. The book remains the foremost bestseller of *Tao Te Ching* versions.

Muller, Charles: TAO TE CHING
New York, Barnes & Noble 2005.
This professor emeritus at the University of Tokyo is a merited translator and expert on East Asian philosophy and religion. He has worked on this clear and straightforward version since 1991, and keeps doing so on his own website.

Red Pine (Bill Porter): LAO TZU'S TAOTECHING
Port Townsend, Copper Canyon Press 1996, 2009.
This version is clever and clear, with a language that feels modern without becoming vulgar. He has avoided punctuation, which makes the reading odd but intriguing. Also included are quotes from famous Chinese commentaries of old for each chapter. The second edition is a revision including the Guodian findings.

Ryden, Edmund: LAOZI: DAODEJING
Oxford University Press 2008.
This version includes the Mawangdui and Guodian findings. The introduction and comments are learned, but the wording in the translation sometimes gives the impression of being dated. Ryden translated *te* as "the life force," which is similar to Arthur Waley's choice of "the power."

Star, Jonathan: TAO TE CHING
New York, Tarcher Penguin 2001.
The subtitle says that this is the definitive edition, which can be discussed. But its material is very rich. The interpretation of the text is given in Star's own words, which often go boldly far from standard versions – but also word by word parallel to the Chinese signs, completely according to the Wang Pi version. It is quite useful to the devoted student of *Tao Te Ching*.

Stenudd, Stefan: TAO TE CHING: THE TAOISM OF LAO TZU EXPLAINED
Malmö, Arriba 2011.
My version is done with consideration of the Mawangdui and Guodian findings. Each chapter is commented. Its translation of *Tao Te Ching* chapters is used frequently as a reference in this book.

Ta-Kao, Chu: TAO TE CHING
London, Mandala 1959.
Ta-Kao allowed himself to rearrange the text according to what he felt was the most probable. That can be discussed. Otherwise, his interpretation is straightforward and clear. The comments are sparse.

Wagner, Rudolf G.: A CHINESE READING OF THE DAODEJING
Albany, State University of New York Press 2003.
This is a translation of the Wang Pi commented version of *Tao Te Ching*, which is the most cherished one in Chinese literature, a classic in its own right. The translation is very competently done, and so are the expert comments. The Chinese text is included. A must for the study of Wang Pi as well as Lao Tzu, but not an easy book to digest.

Waley, Arthur: THE WAY AND ITS POWER
London, Unwin 1934.
Waley's cherished version is assisted by elaborate comments and a long introduction. His interpretations of the chapters are not always the most probable, but his book has won the respect of several important sinologists.

Watts, Alan: TAO: THE WATERCOURSE WAY
New York, Pantheon 1975.

This book was completed and released soon after the demise of Watts. It discussed Taoism with several quotes from *Tao Te Ching* in his own interpretations. Still, the book has made an impact and has been quoted by other texts on Taoism.

Wei, Henry: THE GUIDING LIGHT OF LAO TZU
Wheaton, The Theosophical Publishing House 1982.
This competent and clear version is done with a focus on the mysticism in Lao Tzu's text, rather than the philosophy of it. Still, the version is faithful to the original. Wei's ambition is instead evident in his comments of the chapters and the long introduction.

Wilhelm, Richard: TAO TE CHING
London, Arkana 1985. Translated by H.G. Ostwald.
The first edition of Wilhelm's important interpretation in German was published in 1910. In later editions it was reworked considerably. The comments from 1925 are elaborate about both the language aspects and the ideas of the text. Wilhelm also made a widely spread version of *I Ching*, where he had C. G. Jung write the foreword. It's a pity he didn't do the same with *Tao Te Ching*.

Wing, R. L.: THE TAO OF POWER
New York, Doubleday 1986.
This version includes the Chinese writing, also calligraphy as well as other illustrations of interest. The writer has allowed himself the freedom to adapt some of the wordings to modern concepts, which is not always ideal. The findings in Mawangdui seem not to have been used at all.

Wu, John C. H.: TAO TEH CHING
New York, St. John's University Press 1961.

This competent and straightforward translation is not accompanied with an introduction or comments on the chapters. But it does contain the Chinese text of each chapter.

Yutang, Lin: THE WISDOM OF LAOTSE
New York, Random 1948.
The famous Chinese author made a pleasant interpretation, bordering on religious devotion. The book also contains a quantity of comments and explanations.

Index

A
Aesop 130
Ames, Roger T. 297
Anderson, Rasmus Björn 245
Arnold, Jackie 165
Atkinson, William Walker 281
Augustine 252, 254
Aurelius, Marcus 247

B
Bachman, Margo Shapiro 294
Bach, Richard 273-274
Bahm, Archie J. 94-96, 187-188, 196
Baird, David 52
Balfour, Frederic Henry 297
Barwick, Dee Danner 271
Batty, Roy 216
Beaumont, Francis 262
Beckwith, John W. 270
Blade Runner 216
Blake, Toni 231
Blakney, Raymond B. 297
Blavatsky, Madame 280
Blistein, David 216
Blyth, R. H. 226
Bodhidharma 23
Bodhipaksa 280

Branson, Richard 141, 219
Bredenberg, Jeff 33
Breszny, Rob 202
Bretas, Junia 113-114
Bryce, Derek 83
Buddha 99, 122, 270, 283
Buddhism 17, 23, 74, 105, 122, 124, 132, 205, 279
Buffet, Warren 113
Burwash, Peter 140
Bynner, Witter 26-27, 40, 42, 86-89, 239-240, 297
Byrne, Rhonda 137

C

Campbell, Joseph 30
Carey, Mike 194
Carnegie, Dale 238
Carroll, Sean 231
Carus, Paul 22-23, 298
Chalmers, John 11, 298
Chán 23
Chan, Wing-tsit 33, 63, 92, 179, 185, 206, 298
Chen, Ellen M. 298
Cheney, Sheldon 190-191
Cheng, Man-jan 299
ch'i 52, 64, 102
Chopra, Deepak 242-243
Cleary, Thomas 278, 299
Clever, Linda Hawes 42
Coenn, Daniel 85, 266
Cohen, Alan 118
Collins, Mabel 280
Conellias, David 113
Confucius 111, 144, 178, 185, 263, 278, 282
Coonley, Queene Ferry 190

Cooper, Jean C. 85
Copeland, Pala 253
Cotgrave, Randle 216
Crew, Bud 238
Cromwell, Oliver 246
Crowley, Aleister 299

D

Dale, Ralph Alan 65-67, 114
Dalton, Jerry O. 229
Davis, Miles 84
Dhammapada 98-99
Dolan, John Patrick 263
Donohue, Brian 231
Dowman, Keith 214
Dudek, Louis 281
Dunhuang 74
Duyvendak, J. J. L. 299
Dyer, Wayne W. 81-83, 108-109, 182, 233, 288, 289, 294, 295

E

Ecclesiastes 245, 248
Ekeren, Glenn Van 193
Elliot, Elisabeth 'Betty' 253-254
Els, Paul van 278
English, Jane 97, 118, 132-134, 143, 185, 227, 299

F

Fellini, Federico 36
Feng, Gia-fu 97, 118, 132-134, 143, 185, 227, 299
Ferrini, Paul 42-43
Fielding, Henry 194
Fletcher, John 262
Freke, Timothy 160-161

Frey, James 62
Friedmann, Susan A. 47
Fromm, Erich 154-155
Fuller, Thomas 136-137

G
Gandhi, Mahatma 270
Garascia, Nancy 253
Garcia, Jessie 271
Garcia, Joey 37
Gibbs, Tam C. 299
Gibson, Jack 140
Giles, Herbert A. 256, 300
Giles, Lionel 127, 130
Girling, A. J. 77-79
Gnomologia 136
Godek, Gregory J. P. 52
Gorgias 224
Gove, D. S. 71
Guodian 10, 206, 297, 300, 302, 304, 305
Gurvitch, Georges 72

H
Hale, Gill 257
Hall, David L. 297
Halpern, John H. 216
Havamal 245, 246
Hayward, Susan 148, 233
Heider, John 199-200, 276
Henricks, Robert G. 21, 104, 175, 182, 198, 206, 211, 293, 300
Hibbert, Christina G. 250
Hinduism 105, 124
Hoff, Benjamin 203, 204, 289, 301
Hohne, Kari 162

Hooper, David 231
Howard, Vernon 147, 190, 233
Howell, James 218
Hua, Ellen Kei 172
Hua Hu Ching 69, 73-76, 100, 122-123, 168, 231
Huang, Chungliang Al 30

I
I Ching 146, 162, 172, 299, 306
Ivanhoe, Philip J. 30, 63, 188, 289, 301

J
Jakes, T. D. 46
Jesus 149, 222, 232, 275
Johnson, Dale A. 150-152
Julien, Stanislas 11, 301
Jung, C. G. 306

K
Kang-hu, Kiang 26
Karlgren, Bernhard 109, 239, 286, 301-302
Kawasaki, Guy 46
Kehl, Richard 37
Khaldun, Ibn 137
Khan, Pir Vilayat Inayat 221
King, Deborah 138
Koontz, Dean 56-57
Krum, Charlotte 190
Kuchler, Bonnie Louise 31
kuei 93, 171

L
Lau, D. C. 26, 78, 83, 87, 99, 128, 151, 161, 171, 198, 208, 210, 224, 251, 276, 286, 292, 302

Leary, Timothy 259
Legge, James 13, 21, 29, 50, 65, 83, 88, 96, 111, 133, 144, 164, 172, 185, 187, 191, 196, 205, 223, 233, 239, 240, 244, 256, 268, 272, 282, 286, 297, 302
Le Guin, Ursula 302
Leo, Robert A. 140
Lewis, George 274
Li, Lycke 282
Lincoln, Abraham 9
Lingerman, Hal 155
Link, Al 253
Little, Ruth 219
Lockridge, Norman 156
Loeffler, T. A. 45-46
Long, George 247
Lynch, Jerry 30

M

Macdonnel, David Evans 237
Machiavelli 120
Mackay, Alan 179-180
MacManus, Seumas 194
Mair, Victor H. 120, 133, 303
Malet, Marianne Dora 193
Manalang, Maria 142
Martinet, Jeanne 199
Mascaro, Juan 98
Maule, Emma 221
Maurer, Herrymon 303
Mawangdui 10, 96, 206, 245, 293, 298, 300-306
Medhurst, C. Spurgeon 179
meme 18, 130, 137, 142, 248, 291
Miles, Thomas H. 303
Miller, Maryann 43

Miller, Tony 47
Millman, Dan 37
Milne, A. A. 203
Mitchell, Langdon Elwyn 165
Mitchell, Stephen 20, 22-24, 32, 49, 52, 58-59, 62-63, 82-83, 91-93, 106, 107, 119-121, 124-125, 134, 163-164, 177, 205, 208-209, 247, 250-251, 267-268, 285-286, 288, 303
Moore, Marianne 218-219
More, Hannah 218-219
Muller, Charles 31, 151, 152, 153, 304
mushin 31, 205

N
Nāgārjuna 214
Nakamura, Hajime 180
Ni, Hua-Ching 74-76, 100, 123, 168-169
nirvana 98-99
Noël, Francois 11

O
Oech, Roger von 37
Osho 222-225
O'Toole, Garson 270-271
Outlaw, Frank 270-271

P
Pandit, Sakya 214
Paroimiographia 218
Peter, Laurence J. 130
Pilates, Pontius 222
pinyin 11
Pi, Wang 10, 300, 304-305
p'o 235
Poetics 90

Porter, Bill 304
Potter, Charles Francis 211-212

Q

qi 52, 64, 102
Quigley, Isabel 36

R

Raines, Asya 199
Rajneesh, Bhagwan Shree 222
Ramacharaka, Yogi 280
Randt, Leandie du 55
Rao, Narasingha 137
Raskas, Bernard S. 131
Reade, Charles 270
Red Pine 304
Reilly, Matthew 98
Reisser, Paul C. 242
ren 178, 180
Renzi, Renzo 37
Rico, Yrma 253
Riley, Matthew 99
Roman, Sanaya 242, 294
Run, Rev. 115
Ryan, M. J. 39-41
Ryden, Edmund 304

S

Sasson, Remez 137
satori 241
Seaton, J. P. 302
Seeger, Pete 246
Sellers, Jeff M. 33
Sharma, Narinder 223

Sikes, George 246
Silton, Nava R. 130
Sinatra, Frank 238
Sinha, Shall 263
Smith, Huston 257
Socrates 192
Sorokin, Pitirim 71-72
Star, Jonathan 83, 103, 104, 109, 288, 304
Stenudd, Stefan 305
Stevenson, Jay 99
Svoboda, Melannie 274
Sze, Mai-mai 256

T

t'ai-lao 33
Ta-Kao, Chu 305
te 104, 111, 129, 190, 304
Thatcher, Margaret 270
Theosophy 280, 283
Thomas, Cynthia 114
Ti 167
T'ien Tao 68
Tohei, Koichi 193
Tolle, Eckhart 227
Trismegistus, Hermes 281
Tulku, Tarthang 214
Tyrell, Dr. 216
Tyson, Mike 34
Tzu, Chuang 143-145, 148, 172, 185, 190-191, 231, 233-234, 255-257, 272-273, 299, 302
Tzu, Lieh 256
Tzu, Mo 111-112
Tzu, Wen 278

V

Valeria, Andrea 230
Vane, Sir Henry 246
Vaughan, Frances E. 283
Vitvan 281
Voltaire 156

W

Wade-Giles 11
Wagner, Rudolf G. 305
Waley, Arthur 59, 83, 87, 106, 111, 125, 134, 203, 208, 231, 255-257, 288, 304-305
Walker, Brian Browne 69, 74, 76, 123, 168-169, 231
Walter, Jamie S. 221
Walters, Dottie 263
Watson, Burton 144, 256
Watts, Alan 288, 305
Wendt, George 221
Wieger, Léon 83
Wilde, Oscar 264
Wilhelm, Richard 306
Williams, Virginia and Redford 111
Wing, R. L. 29, 306
Wu, Shelly 157
wu-wei 28, 33, 71, 119, 136, 143, 238-239, 255, 306

Y

yang 52, 64-67, 102
yin 52, 64-67, 102
Yin Fu Ching 191
ying 235
Yousry, Menis 201
Yutang, Lin 50, 179, 230, 307

Z

Zedong, Mao 130
Zen 17, 22-23, 34, 114, 119, 205, 226-227, 239, 241, 248, 257, 279, 281, 283
Zikria, B. A. 184-185
Zubko, Andy 143, 242-243

www.ingramcontent.com/pod-product-compliance
Lightning Source LLC
LaVergne TN
LVHW091625070526
838199LV00044B/937